What Ot.._

The hardest job of an author is to combine a fresh perspective with practical application. In *Created to Make Wealth*, Bob Bertelsen nails it!

You will receive fresh perspectives and practical application on wealth, stewardship, tithing, giving, and spending.

If you read and apply what you learn, this book will change your life forever. I know because it has changed mine.

May the Lord bless you in abundance as you align your finances with His way, truth, and light.

Michael B. Ross
Author, Speaker and Entrepreneur

*****

The biblical message of wealth has been misinterpreted for decades! In *Created to Make Wealth* Bob shares life experiences and keys to walking in God's plan and purpose for wealth. In his book, he takes the truth of God's word and makes it easy to understand and apply to your wealth for you and generations to come. I encourage you to read and share this book with others.

Dr. John Benefiel
Heartland Apostolic Prayer Network
Presiding Apostle

*****

If you are a person who is looking for a path to financial success. And you want to be mentored by someone who has a powerful personal story of exactly that, then you need to read,

Created to Make Wealth. Bob's book is a wonderful combination of his journey to understand the power of generosity and faith. Bob also does a masterful job of explaining the scriptures concerning what is taught in the Bible about finances. You will enjoy his story, moving from faith to freedom in finances. You will also find his book to be very instructional for practical application. The truth regarding finances from Bob's life will thrill and shock you. The practical application for your life will equip you to succeed in your finances and reveal the heart of God's love and provision for your life.

Are you ready to grow in faith? To understand what financial stewardship really is and how the Lord wants to trust you with the treasure of His kingdom? If so, this is a must-read. Do it and prepare for the journey of a lifetime.

Dr. Charles F. Hamilton
President, Harvest Preparation Int. Ministry

*****

Created to Make Wealth is an inspirational story of how God used a simple man who could barely graduate from high school and molded him into a financier of the Kingdom. Along the way, Bob shares very practical keys to success in good times and in bad. If you have ever wondered why God gave you a desire to create wealth, this book is a must-read.

Perry Chickonoski
Pastor, Real Living Ministries
Co-Leader HAPN Economy Mountain

*****

I am very excited about this book. It needs to be in the hands of every business person. Wealth can be equally as burdensome as poverty without generosity. Bob's insights into stewardship move the reader into a mindset of generosity, which leads to true wealth. Bob Bertelsen lives this book. He is generous, knows his wealth serves a bigger purpose, and God has truly blessed him for it.

Joy Chickonoski
Founder and Executive Director of Unleashed Healing Center
Co-Leader of Real Living Ministries Apostolic Center
National Apostolic Leader for Heartland Apostolic Prayer Network

*****

The greatest tool used against the Body of Christ by the enemy is deception. Unfortunately, those deceived do not recognize the deception because it is wrapped in religious teachings or wrong mindsets. In Bob Bertelsen's book, he tells his life story, doing an excellent job of bringing revelation truth to those deceptions. In his simple easy steps to take our place as Stewards and as Financiers of the Kingdom, he has given us usable tools to overcome the deception. It is a must-read for all our HAPN leaders.

Dr. Yolanda McCune
HAPN Kingdom Culture Director

*****

I found Bob's book to be enjoyable, applicable, a quick read and timely for today's businessman. Like Bob, I am not one prone to read a lot, and when I do, I want the information to be direct and of immediate value. I have always been a believer in the benefits of the tithe. Bob's belief in the tithing of the business is one that I wish had been presented to me earlier in my career before my retirement. I believe that it would have blessed my business, the ministry and myself greatly. This is a concept that will benefit many. I will forward this book to my sons. I trust that you will enjoy Bob's book as much as I did."

Gary McCune
President, Camco Home Improvement Inc. (Retired)
Immediate Past Chair, Stillwater Chamber of Commerce
Past Chair, Oklahoma Association of Electric Cooperatives
Past Chair/current Vice-Chair, Central Electric Cooperative
Past Chair, Stillwater Home Builders Association

*****

Created to Make Wealth is not your typical book about money. This book covers everything from spiritual principles to practical advice. Through stories from his own life and deep insights, Bob Bertelsen uses the Bible's own teachings to challenge common ideas about wealth, resources, and possessions.

Chris Holm
Pastor, Upper Room Fellowship

*****

I felt this book told a compelling story and used God's word to help us understand the importance and rewards of becoming a better steward. I really enjoyed that each notion was backed up by God's scripture. I've learned a lot from this book and truly believe it's changed my personal understanding of good stewardship."

Nick Sukosd
Operations Manager, A Plus Powder Coaters, Inc.

*****

An easy to read guide that I thoroughly enjoyed! These techniques can be applied to any financial status. This book is a wonderful reminder to let God take the lead, especially in our finances!

Wayne Morris
Quality Manager, A Plus Powder Coaters, Inc.

*****

Bob Bertelsen is a man of his word; he not only talks the talk but also walks the walk. Bob shows this by putting God first in everything he does, and on several occasions, I have heard him say that his employees are his greatest assets in his business.

When a businessman honors God and takes care of his employees the way he does, it is no wonder Bob excels at business.

Created to Make Wealth is engaging, quick to read, and full of scenarios that make it easy to relate to.

Melanie Sprouse
Administrative Assistant, A Plus Powder Coaters, Inc.

*****

This book was truly an inspiring read. Not only did it transform my way of thinking, but my husband's also.

We learned to be financially successful in our lives, you cannot be spiritually bankrupt. God must be present and forefront in everything we do. As Bob demonstrated in his book, without God, we truly have nothing.

Heather Reilly
Office Manager, A Plus Powder Coaters, Inc.

*****

For as long as I have known Bob, he goes after God and what God has created him to do. Bob is comfortable in his own skin and yet allows God to adjust that skin as He sees fit. He does live up to every word he has said in this book; according to his own advice and God's direction. If you want to be a financier of the Kingdom, heed Bob's advice.

Laurie Bertelsen
Wife of over 36 years

*****

Bob has been a trusted friend, boss and business mentor to me for over 20 years. The faith, wisdom, knowledge and business insights reflected in this book have allowed him to create wealth and leave an enormous kingdom footprint. I am confident that they can do the same for you.

Terry Watson
Sales Manager, A Plus Powder Coaters, Inc.

*****

Being a life-long, personal friend, I knew Bob when his first "Vette" was a basic 1980 Chevette and he lived in a trailer park. And before that in high school when his tricked-out GMC pickup truck owned him. I've watched how God has reshaped Bob from the inside out as he was receptive to "wisdom from above." Consequently, I've also witnessed his wealth growing, right alongside a joy in outrageous generosity that mirrors heaven's. I encourage you to let your own life be transformed by his insights.

Bruce Stryffeler
Business owner, Pastor, Upper Room Fellowship

*****

Created to Make Wealth is a combination of a heart for God, His people, His plans and the spiritually practical ways and means of walking with Him in our daily lives to accomplish in the natural what He has promised by His Spirit. It is foundational to the rest of life.

Camy "Cameron" Arnett
Actor/Speaker/Director/Producer/Minister/
Author/Activist/Entrepreneur

Bob Bertelsen has been a friend and mentor to me for over 20 years. He has helped grow my business and was influential in my salvation. His insights and wisdom in business and finances have been a huge help in growing my business.

Robert Pyatt
CEO RC Fabricating

*****

Full of wisdom and advice in so many areas, this book gets better with each chapter. Bob stretches the reader to see beyond finances and wealth as the world has come to understand it. His personal stories combined with really practical lessons makes for an engaging read that continues to affect you long after you finish the book!

Kate Holm
Pastor Upper Room Fellowship

Created

to

MAKE

Wealth

BOB BERTELSEN

Copyright

Dedication

I FIRST DEDICATE THIS BOOK to my Lord and Savior. If it was not for God, I don't believe I would be alive today or have ever made any wealth. My wealth comes from him, not my own abilities. Without God I am nothing.

I want to thank my wife, Laurie, for standing with me all these years. She has been an encourager and supporter of me in all our business endeavors. Her prayers and love are priceless.

I want to thank Mark LaMoncha, Phil Steiner and Jim Poma for their support when I first got into business. They are valuable resources to me.

I want to thank Pastors Joy & Perry Chickonoski for their spiritual covering and encouragement to finish this book. Also, Pastor Chuck Hamilton for his encouragement and support when I attended his church.

Thank you to Faisal Malick for helping me bring this book to print. You are a valuable resource to me and I thank you.

Contents

First Foreword
by Faisal Malick

IT IS AN HONOR TO INTRODUCE BOB BERTELSEN and his epic new book *Created to Make Wealth.*

Bob brings a down to earth message about heavens economy with practical insights anyone can apply. He reminds the reader of their God-given ability to create wealth and its true purpose.

Bertelsen pulls back the curtain on his personal journey of faith into the discovery of God's plan concerning wealth & finance without leaving out the pitfalls along the way. Whether he is on the race track or in the market place Bob sees himself as an ordinary guy with an extraordinary God.

His message is real and powerful, reaching beyond the veil of religious mindsets that cloud the potential and intent of Kingdom wealth.

He's not afraid to remind the business owner, layman or stay at home mother that no matter your current state, you have God's economy at your fingertips and access to His Kingdom strategies for wealth.

I encourage you to get comfortable and journey through this book with an open heart and mind ready to embrace the God-given potential of wealth creation hidden in you!

Well done Bob!!

Faisal Malick,
President, The Plumbline Network
Plumblinenetwork.com
Lead Pastor, Covenantoflife.org

Second Foreword
by Dr. Harold R. Eberle

THE KINGDOM OF GOD NEEDS PEOPLE like Bob Bertelsen. It needs financiers of the Kingdom. It needs people of God who are created to make wealth and know how to steward it.

In my 40+ years of ministry, I've seen a lot of things, gone many places, taken the power of God into dark corners of spiritual wastelands. In so doing, I've put my life on the line in dangerous countries. I've opened myself to strangers, trusting in the Spirit's leading, been exposed to hostile fire, literally needing sharpshooters around me as I preached to hungry masses.

I'm not alone. There are tens of thousands of us called to do exceptional things for God. Missionaries, traveling ministers, church planters, healers, intercessors. They are people who surrender their right to earn a living so life can be brought to others in need. We are the spearheads, the tools that breach the boundary between God's dominion and darkness. We are thrust into places, spiritually and physically, that the average Christian has never dreamed of. Forget the fanciful Christian novels of great exploits and spiritual adventures. We live it, day in and day out.

People aggrandize the image of fulltime ministry. Perhaps they crave foreign travel or spiritual intrigue. Some imagine the glorious moments when the dead rise, the deaf hear or cancer victims spit out the last of their disease, but they don't know our struggles, our lack, how we charge into withering fire while praying desperately that the support troops are following close behind.

Yet not everyone is called to kiss their family goodbye, climb in a plane and spend the next six months laying a godly foundation in some hell hole of humanity that few even thought had a prayer of a chance. Yet the eyes of the grateful inhabitants say it all: "We are so glad you came. You brought God to us. When will you return?"

This is my life and the lives of many. But we can't do it alone. For every minute we spend on the mission field or in the local church, hundreds of thousands of God's people are at work in support of our efforts. Intercessors are praying, editors are refining our words, business people are launching into new territories, and people are going to work: secretaries, engineers, ranchers, farmers, doctors, nurses, cooks, software developers, mechanics, plumbers and astronomers are all working to make ministry possible.

We're the folks at the delivery end of this ministerial missile, but people like Bob are at the propulsion end. We can't get on a jet without money for the ticket. We can't launch a water system in Kenya unless it's donated. We can't feed the poor in soup kitchens unless the food is grown, harvested, supplied and prepared. We're the mouthpieces, the frontline soldiers, the hands on the ladles passing out broth. But we must have your backing.

This is why God was so prescriptive in how we are to give of our resources and steward that with which He entrusts us.

Bob lays it out simply. The Gospel moves on financing. Yes, it moves through prayer, talent, training, development and integrity. Take any of those away and the system breaks down. But the Gospel also moves on money.

People love stories of the Gospel in action: thousands upon thousands saved in open-air outreaches, grinning natives holding fat children in front of straw huts, clean water flowing into villages, green crops standing tall.

Well, here is the rest of the story. It starts with finances. Unless you give of your time, your love, your heart and your money, the gospel will not get far. You are the key.

So give...

In ways you haven't dreamed.

So give...

A dollar, a sandwich, a ride to a friend, a doctor bill.

So give...

A tithe, an offering, a sacrifice.

It starts with the knowledge of God's will followed by obedience and rewards. It yields the peace of knowing that you are right with God in all aspects of your life.

See, the lives of those earning wealth are as vital to the Kingdom of God as the ministers depending on that wealth. The giving is to be a result of God's blessing. Seek God for greater resources for giving. But be ready to take the first steps, even when things look dire. Consider this: if you are reluctant to give because finances are tight, could it be that they are tight because...you need to start giving?

"Test me in this," says the Lord Almighty.

Jump into God's river of finances. This mighty stream doesn't stand still. It flows into your life, surrounds you and continues on. It's an irresistible force for good, but you must remove the impediments. Release your faith in God's goodness. Stagnant water is soon stale. The life is in the flow.

Join us. At work, at home, in gatherings, by the light of early morning. Learn God's ways of giving. Your ministry just might be the numbers you put on a check.

I can't promise that you'll never have another financial challenge. But here's what I can promise. Somewhere in the world is a man or woman on their knees in a rude shelter, praying in the wee hours before sunrise that the ministry they are about to undertake will reach the people desperate for redemption. The clothes on their back, the gas in their tank and the meal to start their day comes from you—the givers, the workers, the obedient, the stewards of God's resources.

For you who yearn for glory, for hind's feet on high places, for fiery demons quenched by God's angels, for souls cleansed by the light of the Gospel, here's your dream fulfilled: Give...and it shall be given unto you.

Bob Bertelsen tells us how to steward wealth. He tells us to be free in our giving and to love the God who gives in return. The blessings of God are meant to reward us, to confirm our paths, and to enable us to share the riches of His Kingdom with the world.

We are all in this as one. Let us break bread together and see the glory of the Kingdom of God arising on the Earth.

Thank you,

Dr. Harold R. Eberle
Worldcast Ministry and Publishing

Introduction

I HAVE HAD WRITING A BOOK ON FINANCES on my heart for many years. Every time I think about finances and what God would have me say, he adds something more. I originally thought it would be a book on stewardship or God's favor. But when I started writing and reading what I had written, it seemed to change to more about finances and the fact that I was created to make wealth.

Now there are some who might struggle with the statement: "I was created to make wealth." Yet Deuteronomy 8:18 NIV says:

> But remember the Lord your God, for it is he who gives you the ability to produce wealth, and so confirms his covenant, which he swore to your ancestors, as it is today.

God gave us the ability to produce wealth. In my life, I have lived this scripture long before I ever read it. God showed me over twenty years ago that I was to be a financer of the Kingdom. "A what?" you might ask. A financer of the Kingdom is someone who brings the finances to a ministry for the ministry to not only survive but flourish. No ministry can exist without money.

I knew my calling was to make wealth and honor God with it. I also realized I am not the only one created to make wealth. I believe there are thousands, if not tens of thousands, of men and women of God who are called to make wealth.

This book is about what I have learned along the way—what I believe to be a godly perspective of money and how we should handle it. The bottom line is this: If we can't handle the finances we currently have, how can God entrust us with more? I believe there are five keys to making wealth and honoring God with it. I want to give you those keys and the insight into what you need to do to advance in your wealth quest. You are about to read what I have done, some good, some not so good. It is my journey to becoming a financer of the Kingdom, as one who honors God with his wealth and assets.

I was created to make wealth. You were created to make wealth. Let's explore how to do it.

1

Fast and Impulsive

IT WAS AUGUST 2013. I was with "Brute Force," my custom-built '71 Camaro. With a modified LS7 engine pushing 650HP through a six-speed transmission, it feared nothing. We were at the Northeast Muscle Car Challenge—an event I hosted annually. It's strictly for American-made, V8 muscle cars, preferably 1987 and older. No front-wheel-drive, no drifting, no street racing through Hong Kong. Just God bless American muscle.

I adjusted my shoulder harness, tightened my helmet strap, snapped the Hans device to my helmet, and waited to start my track session. There were a few clouds against a blue horizon. I was thanking God for perfect racing weather when the grid worker released me to go, launching me into a 1.6 mile, 12-turn riot of smoke and squealing tires.

My memory of that day begins at turn seven—a blind, 90-degree that dropped off to the right. You had to trust the turn-in cone on the left as the turn didn't reveal itself until you were fully committed. Never one for half measures, I threw the steering wheel hard right and the Camaro dropped onto the inside apron in perfect placement. Sensing my fastest lap so far, I powered out of the turn, buried the gas and felt the joy of 650 horses rising to the challenge.

I slammed into 4th gear and let the engine rip as I headed to turn eight, a left-hand sweeper. It was a bit more forgiving, so with engine unleashed and no hint of brakes, I caught the apron and flew up the short back straight.

The speedo read 138 mph as turn nine, a right-hand dogleg rushed up to greet me. I tapped the brakes to set the front end, scrubbing a bit of speed as well. Maybe it was the thrill of the hunt, I don't know, but I was a heartbeat late on the wheel and left a few extra ponies to handle the inside corner.

Brute Force responded by pushing to the outside edge of the turn while my harness held me against the G-forces. Peering out the left window revealed a thin ribbon of asphalt between my tires and soft grass. A precarious position, for sure. Physics is a relentless opponent. Hearing the siren's song of squealing tires, I reassured myself:

"I got this. I got this."

My muscle car was in a four-wheel drift and rapidly closing the margin between awesomeness and disaster. Then it happened. Two wheels dropped off the track and succumbed to the ruinous turf. Nothing good ever comes from tires meeting grass. I resigned myself to the outcome of this hastily arranged union. Brute Force and I were on the ride of our lives.

We spun 180 degrees and converted our momentum to setting the track record for racing in reverse. Sliding backward, I crossed the track to the infield. All I could see were guardrails in both side mirrors. Not particularly encouraging. In a moment of clarity, I did what any good Christian race car driver would do.

"Jesus, Jesus, Jesus. HELP ME!"

Not my most eloquent prayer, but I was pressed for time.

Calculating the odds, I knew that if I hit the wall, I'd be ok...sort of. In a microburst of memory, I relived the months I spent building Brute Force in my garage. I knew every inch of that car, every panel, every brace and frame member. Heck, I knew

2

each bolt and its torque value. As we slid into oblivion, I was confident the car would protect me, but would it be destroyed in the process? My eternal life was secure through Jesus Christ, but Brute Force? I could only hope he had gotten saved somewhere along the way.

I braced for the imminent arrival of the guard rail but it never came. Instead, it slid along in a blur just a few feet off the left side of the car.

What, no impact?

"Thank you, Jesus! Thank you, Jesus!"

Still sliding, we crossed the track above turn ten and came to rest on a grassy knoll. When I finally pried my fingers from the wheel, I thanked God one more time then drove to the pit lane just a hundred yards away to regroup.

Miraculously, there was no damage except the pucker mark in the seat and my wounded pride. It was a great day to be alive. Any wreck you walk away from is a good one.

My Beginnings

My passion for cars started at an early age with matchbox cars and then plastic models. I customized the models, cutting them up and reassembling them to my liking. Using paper clips and card stock, I figured out how to hinge the doors. Of course, no model car is complete without spark plug wires and dipsticks in the motors.

I bought my first real vehicle at 16—a 1976 GMC 4wd pickup truck. It was a black beauty with a red interior, and I was hopelessly in love. As with my plastic models, I couldn't leave it stock. After a lift kit, oversized wheels and tires, I painted it black and added custom painted stripes. (Everyone knows it's the stripes that make it fast.) A four-way power seat out of a luxury car gave it the necessary comfort for long trips, and an overhead console with speakers and lights was the touch of class that turned heads. The final add was an external roll bar and a row of floodlights arrayed like blackbirds on a wire. Two thousand candlepower was all we needed to turn nighttime into a lifetime.

I've built many cars after that, but it wasn't until 2008 that I fell in love with racing. You see, I had built a show car in 2002 that had been in every magazine, won many awards, including Grand Champion of the Street Machine Nationals. But despite the fame and accolades, I quickly bored of car shows. Sitting by the masterpieces I'd built, talking to strangers as they drifted by, answering the same questions over and over again...I was growing restless. Apparently, I was into the building, not the showing.

It was at a Good Guys show that I first saw autocross, an event where a car is driven through a sea of cones and competitively timed. The cars have to handle exceptionally well, accelerate quickly and stop on a dime. I took a ride in Kyle Tucker's car from Detroit Speed and I was hooked. However, when I took my show car to the track, it did terribly. The car was not designed for performance and I didn't understand driving. All beauty and no muscle or brains.

I resolved to build a car that would look like a show car and function like a race car. In time, owing to my penchant for great-looking performance, my race cars could also compete in car shows. As my skills progressed, I graduated from driving autocross to also competing in road racing. I have improved quite a bit since I first started racing and now place or win many events each year.

THE HEART OF THE RACER

I race because I love it. The adrenaline rush, my heart singing with every turn, the comradery of likeminded gearheads, all make the investment worth it. That's the point, generally. Wrecking a $250,000 custom-built muscle car is not high on anyone's agenda.

In our finances, we have times that drive our hearts with excitement. Our adrenaline flows and we are stoked. When buying our first car, putting a down payment on a house or paying off a crushing debt, exercising our financial muscle can be exhilarating. Yet there are also times when we power into a curve thinking "I got this," only to find out it's got us. For many people, finances bring anxiety, misery, even ruin. Let us remember, however, that the same God who guides our lives can also guide our finances...if we allow him. For the Christian—the believer in Christ—there is more to managing our wealth than throwing up a prayer and saying "Bless me, Jesus!"

We were created by God to *make* wealth. I'd like to show you how...and why.

2

Crisis and Calling

ABOUT TWENTY YEARS AGO, I was facing a financial crisis. Now you're probably thinking:

Was Bob having trouble making ends meet?

Did all those expensive cars break the bank?

Was he going out of business?

Did the bank foreclose on his home?

Did the IRS force him to file bankruptcy?

His wife finally left him, eh?

Strange how we always assume the worst...as we define *worst*. Well, this will surprise you, but my financial situation wasn't due to a lack of money, and my marriage was thriving. Our problem was that we had *too much* money.

OK, I get it. What's the crisis in too much money? Don't they write songs about "no such thing as too much money"? Yes, they do. And they make good money on those songs. My situation was a little different, however.

Many things were running through my mind as I surveyed my growing bank account. For starters, the church seems to imply that you have to give up every material thing to be closer to God, that a poverty mindset makes you holy and righteous. The less you possess, the godlier you become, right? Hey, it worked for all those monks during the middle ages.

This viewpoint is not without scriptural support.

Again I tell you, it is easier for a camel to go through the eye of a needle than for someone who is rich to enter the kingdom of God.

Matthew 19:24 NIV

Jesus answered, "If you want to be perfect, go, sell your possessions and give to the poor, and you will have treasure in heaven. Then come, follow me."

Matthew 19:21 NIV

For the love of money is a root of all kinds of evil. Some people, eager for money, have wandered from the faith and pierced themselves with many griefs.

1 Timothy 6:10 NIV

Reading about the camel and the eye of a needle sent shivers down my spine. You see, my wife and I had a nice home, two nice cars and cash in the bank. I was so far from that needle that it haunted me.

God, am I going to hell because I have money in the bank?

I wanted to know my godly calling in life. Discovering your calling was a popular point of discussion in Christian circles at the time. *What is your purpose? What are you doing for God?*

To me, having a call of God on my life sounded like being a pastor or a missionary. That was serving God, in my mind, and I didn't want either of those callings.

I wrestled with these issues for a long time, praying and asking God to show me his calling for me. In the spirit of full surrender, I told God that if he wanted me to be a missionary or pastor, I would do it, but it wasn't what I really wanted to do.

Personally, I rated my success factor for either of these callings in the single digits. Still, nothing definitive came to me.

I finally took a different tack in my search for peace. I asked God for answers to my wealth problem. That's when he began to speak to me. He showed me the scripture in Matthew:

> As evening approached, there came a rich man from Arimathea, named Joseph, who had himself become a disciple of Jesus.

Matthew 27:57 NIV

I noticed something odd about the man in this verse. He was a *rich man* who was also a *disciple of Jesus*.

Wait a minute, God. I must have read that wrong. That has to be a typo or something. That word "rich" probably means spiritually rich, right?

Yet as I read it over and over, I realized that Jesus had wealthy disciples. Most people have heard of the twelve disciples (later the apostles), but the Bible tells us there were other disciples as well who followed Jesus, and many of these had money. With this realization, a peace about my bank account began to creep into my soul.

MONK AND MERCHANT

In 2005, Terry Felber published a book that changed my life: *The Legend of the Monk and the Merchant.* Dave Ramsey, the renowned Christian financial teacher, sent a copy of the book to all his financial peace administrators. My salesman for our business, A Plus Powder Coaters Inc., Terry Watson, is a financial peace administrator. He teaches a class on the subject at our company and at area churches. Terry came to me one day and said, "Bob, you have to read this book. It's you."

Now, in all candor, I should tell you I am not a good academic student. I don't read much and I retain even less. I struggled to pass high school. I was half a credit short of graduation and the school board held a special meeting to vote me through. They didn't want me back any more than I wanted to come back.

The fact that this book was in the form of a story, however, piqued my interest. It was about a grandfather telling his grandson how he had become the businessman he is today. As children, he and his best friend planned to become monks when they grew up. The grandfather's friend did become a monk, but the grandfather decided to become a merchant. This caused a rift between the two men since the monk believed that a poverty lifestyle was necessary to be close to God.

Later in life, the two reconnected. The monk had read in the Book of Revelations that God calls us to be kings and priests. Kings have money and priests spread the word. The monk now saw both functions as godly callings to ministry, forming a partnership. The grandfather and monk rekindled their friendship and became united in their callings.

Moving Forward

God was showing me that he had +created me to make wealth. This was a paradigm shift for me. Suddenly, I had a calling. I was to make wealth! And I was already walking in it! As I thought about this, however, I realized God created me not just to *make* wealth but to be a financer of the Kingdom.

When this revelation hit me, I began to share the good news with others. "Hey, guess what! God created me to be a financer of the Kingdom!"

Not surprisingly...it didn't go over really well. Most people looked at me like I had three heads. Some readers, too, may be wondering what I mean by a financer of the Kingdom (or maybe I really do have three heads). Please allow me to explain.

I realized that no church, ministry or missionary can do anything without money. Lacking financial resources, churches close their doors, ministries fold and missionaries stay home.

My calling, as I understood it, was to partner with missionaries, ministries and churches (our church in particular) as a financer. You see, their destinies cannot be fulfilled without money. By me and my wife, Laurie, partnering with them, it fulfills their destinies and our destiny. It's a win/win for both of us. I now knew that my calling was to be a financer of the kingdom.

I finally was at peace. I could work in business, which is what I loved and excelled at. I could be wealthy and be a disciple of Jesus. No longer was I a camel straining to get through the eye of a needle! And I could further the Kingdom of God with my talents and abilities, which were in the area of finances.

I was ecstatic. And while the story of the monk and the merchant crystalized what I had been thinking and doing for several years, I knew there was more to share. I want others to catch the vision and understand what I do because they may be called to do something similar. I have distributed hundreds of copies of Felber's book over the years, but it is time to share my story as well.

What I am about to share is the fruit of forty years of discovery. Christian business people, impressed with the success they see, often approach me and ask what I've done to get there. As I have thought about it over the years, I have come up with five key things that have positioned me to allow God to bless us financially. I believe anyone who grasps these simple truths will be positioned for wealth.

As you read, you may think *That is too easy*, or *I already do that*. Yet it's not about applying *some* truths, but *all* of them. None of them are hard if you trust in God.

> *To Him who loved us and washed us from our sins in His own blood, and has made us kings and priests to His God and Father, to Him be glory and dominion forever and ever. Amen.*

> Revelation 1:5-6

3

Wealth

PROSPERITY, MONEY, RICHES, FINANCIAL RESOURCES... What are we talking about? Dollars in the bank, a house on a hill, a bustling factory working 24/7, a stable of classic cars—all are forms of wealth.

Wealth, definition: "an abundance of valuable possessions or money."

As Christians, we walk with God. We trust our eternal lives to him. In the process, we learn to trust everything else to him as well. God is patient, kind, forgiving and instructive. "And yet I will show you the most excellent way," (1 Corinthians 12:31 NIV). As we grow, he shows us how to live and enjoy the blessings of his presence, and that includes wealth.

We will take a deeper look at wealth and its place in a believer's life. Some of this may seem strange at first. So, let me encourage you to keep an open mind and let go of any preconceived ideas you might have about being rich or poor, or even what these terms mean.

CONFRONTING A POVERTY MINDSET

Since I understood that I was created to make wealth, I struggled with the prevailing Christian teachings promoting poverty as holiness, that a lack of financial resources makes a person more spiritual. I am not sure where these beliefs came from—perhaps they were created to make poor people feel better about being poor—but they are patently false.

Having wealth is scriptural, indeed, it pleases God. Certainly, there are times in everyone's life when we face a lack of necessities. Sometimes, a period of lack is God's way of getting our trust away from our financial resources and back on him. However, saying we should be continually poor is like saying we should continually starve ourselves to gain the blessings of a fast.

Let's look at the planks of such teachings, uncover the misunderstandings, and understand what God really intends for us.

THE ROOT

I have heard many people say, "Money is the root of all evil." Unfortunately, this is a frequent misquote. The Bible actually says:

For the love of money is a root of all kinds of evil.

1 Timothy 6:10 NIV (emphasis added)

It is *the love of money*, not money itself, that is *a root of all kinds of evil*. Further, this love is not *the* root of evil, as in singular, but *a* root—one of several. There are many roots to evil. The love of money makes money our god, and this becomes one root of evil. In fact, the love of anything above Father God makes that thing a god, and as such, it becomes sin.

The Bible tells us:

No man can serve two masters: for either he will hate the one, and love the other; or else he will hold to the one, and despise the other. You cannot serve God and mammon.

Matthew 6:24

The definition of mammon is "wealth regarded as an evil influence or false object of worship and devotion."

14

I like The Passion Translation of this verse.

> *How could you worship two gods at the same time? You will have to hate one and love the other, or be devoted to one and despise the other. You can't worship the true God while enslaved to the god of money!"*

Matthew 6:24 TPT

Wow! We can be enslaved to *the god of money*. Sounds awful, doesn't it? We have to make sure that God is high above money or anything else. As Christians, we worship God, not money.

In Luke 4, Jesus was being tempted by the devil to worship him instead of the Father. Jesus' reply to his tempter was succinct.

> *Jesus replied, "The Scriptures say, 'You must worship the Lord your God and serve only him.'"*

Luke 4:8 NLT

The Bible is telling us to worship the Lord our God and serve only him. That means we have to guard against loving and worshiping money.

Mammon is a spirit—a god if we make it such—that can rest on money. However, money can also have a *godly* spirit on it. In that sense, money can be godly or ungodly, although it is our perspective of money and what we do with it that determines whether it is godly or ungodly.

So, what decides whether we are treating our financial resources in a godly or ungodly way? The answer is found in the extent that we are focused on wealth.

Do you believe that:

- if you only had more money, everything would be ok?
- money can fix all your problems?
- if you had more money, you would have less stress?

If you answered *Yes* to these questions, you might be subtly worshipping mammon—the god of money.

The Word of God tells us that we cannot serve God and money. Only one of them can be first in our lives. If God is the one we truly love and worship, we have the right perspective of money. Of course, money itself is not evil. It is our trust in it, our love of money, that makes it evil.

WEALTHY PEOPLE IN SCRIPTURE

Previously, we discussed Joseph, the rich man who was a disciple of Jesus. Joseph offered his hand-hewn tomb for Jesus' burial. Note the qualifier: hand-hewn. In those days, only the super-rich had hand-hewn tombs. Now, we are not talking rich like doctors, lawyers, CEOs and amateur race car drivers. No, we are talking rich like Warren Buffet, Bill Gates, and half of Saudi Arabia. Let's face the facts—a billionaire was a disciple of Jesus.

> *Now when evening had come, there came a rich man from Arimathea, named Joseph, who himself had also become a disciple of Jesus. This man went to Pilate and asked for the body of Jesus. Then Pilate commanded the body to be given to him. When Joseph had taken the body, he wrapped it in a clean linen cloth, and laid it in his new tomb which he had hewn out of the rock; and he rolled a large stone against the door of the tomb, and departed.*
>
> Matthew 27:57-60

Rich people are found throughout the Bible. Let's look at Hezekiah, a man of God and the 13th king of Judah.

> *Hezekiah was very wealthy and highly honored. He built special treasury buildings for his silver, gold, precious stones, and spices, and for his shields and other valuable items. He also constructed many storehouses for his grain, new wine, and olive oil; and he made many stalls for his cattle and pens for his flocks of sheep and goats. He built many towns and acquired vast flocks and herds, for God had given him great wealth.*

> 2 Chronicles 32:27-29 NLT

God gave Hezekiah great wealth and he served God with integrity. This begs the question: How can wealth be bad if it comes from God? Scripture is clearly telling us that wealth that comes from God is good.

Of course, people point to Jesus as the epitome of poverty-based spirituality. After all, he is famous for saying "Foxes have dens and birds have nests, but the Son of Man has no place to lay his head" (Luke 9:58 NIV). Well, Jesus may not have had a bed, but that doesn't mean he was poor.

Consider the evidence in the gospel of Luke just a few verses prior.

> *When the apostles returned, they reported to Jesus what they had done. Then he took them with him and they withdrew by themselves to a town called Bethsaida, but the crowds learned about it and followed him. He welcomed them and spoke to them about the kingdom of God, and healed those who needed healing.*

Late in the afternoon the Twelve came to him and said, "Send the crowd away so they can go to the surrounding villages and countryside and find food and lodging, because we are in a remote place here."

He replied, "You give them something to eat."

They answered, "We have only five loaves of bread and two fish—unless we go and buy food for all this crowd." (About five thousand men were there.)

Luke 9:10-14 NIV

Jesus challenged his disciples to provide dinner for this gathering of hungry followers. Note their response: *unless we go buy food for all this crowd.*

If Jesus and the disciples were poor, how could they even contemplate buying food to feed 5,000 men, plus roughly 5,000 women and 10,000 children? That is a minimum of 20,000 people. Yet the disciples were ready to go buy happy meals for everyone. Can you imagine the cost?

In modern terms, a $5 meal for each person would be $100,000. Not a cheap date. But the disciples didn't say anything about not having enough money to do that. Instead, they spoke as if it was the only alternative.

One can safely assume, then, that they had funds available, and that they were questioning *the means* to carry out Jesus' directive to "give them something to eat."

WHERE YOUR TREASURER IS

Here's another indication of the wealth Jesus and his disciples carried. They had their own treasurer. Only those with large amounts of funds to manage need a treasurer. Such was Jesus' ministry.

> *When Judas had eaten the bread, Satan entered into him. Then Jesus told him, "Hurry and do what you're going to do." None of the others at the table knew what Jesus meant. Since <u>Judas was their treasurer</u>, some thought Jesus was telling him to go and pay for the food or to give some money to the poor. So Judas left at once, going out into the night.*

John 13:27-30 NLT (emphasis added)

Judas was the treasurer. Some translations say that Judas was in charge of the money. The point is that Jesus and his disciples needed someone to hold and manage their money. This implies that they had money that needed to be managed—big money.

FINANCIAL SUPPORTERS

Have you ever wondered where Jesus got his money or resources? Consider this passage:

> *After this, Jesus traveled about from one town and village to another, proclaiming the good news of the kingdom of God. The Twelve were with him, and also some women who had been cured of evil spirits and diseases: Mary (called Magdalene) from whom seven demons had come out; Joanna the wife of Chuza, the manager of Herod's household; Susanna; and many others. These women were helping to support them out of their own means.*

Luke 8:1-3 NIV

Who were these women: Mary, Joanna, and Susanna who were helping to support Jesus and the disciples out of their own means?

Joanna was the wife of Chuza, who managed the household of Herod Antipas—the son of Herod the Great, the violent and ambitious head of Judea. Herod Antipas was quite wealthy, and we can be sure that whoever was managing his household was wealthy as well. Essentially, Joanna was an upper-class, affluent woman who had the means to support Jesus' ministry.

Mary Magdalene came from the area of Magdala, a wealthy fishing and textile community. Mary may have come from an affluent family or been a business owner. Consider the following:

> *Then Mary took about a pint of pure nard, an expensive perfume; she poured it on Jesus' feet and wiped his feet with her hair. And the house was filled with the fragrance of the perfume.*

> John 12:3 NIV

Scholars believe this was Mary Magdalene, and that the perfume cost a year's wage for the average Hebrew worker. She must have had substantial financial resources to acquire this expensive fragrance. Laurie, my wife, has some nice perfumes, but nothing costing $30,000. Mary Magdalene would have been of the upper class in society to spend an average year's wage on perfume.

We don't know anything more about Susanna, but since she is numbered among those who supported the ministry out of her means, one can assume that she had the means to do so.

Remember the rich man from Arimathea named Joseph? The Bible tells us he was a disciple of Jesus. We can assume he was a supporter of Jesus' ministry as well. He and these women were financers of the Kingdom. They partnered with Jesus to meet the needs of the ministry. In so doing, they fulfilled both Jesus' destiny and their destinies.

Some of the disciples were also men of wealth. Four of them owned fishing businesses. Simon (called Peter), and Andrew, James and John were prominent fishermen of Galilee. Most business people I know have considerable financial resources.

It is noteworthy that just before calling these fishermen to follow him, Jesus blessed them with an abundance of fish—a considerable financial blessing that most likely carried them into ministry.

> *[Jesus] said to Simon, "Put out into deep water, and let down the nets for a catch."*
>
> *Simon answered, "Master, we've worked hard all night and haven't caught anything. But because you say so, I will let down the nets."*
>
> *When they had done so, they caught such a large number of fish that their nets began to break. So they signaled their partners in the other boat to come and help them, and they came and filled both boats so full that they began to sink.*
>
> *When Simon Peter saw this, he fell at Jesus' knees and said, "Go away from me, Lord; I am a sinful man!" For he and all his companions were astonished at the catch of fish they had taken, and so were James and John, the sons of Zebedee, Simon's partners.*

> *Then Jesus said to Simon, "Don't be afraid; from now on you will fish for people." So they pulled their boats up on shore, left everything and followed him.*

Luke 5:4-11 NIV (emphasis added)

Then there is Matthew, who had been a tax collector before becoming a disciple. Men of that occupation were known for being very wealthy.

There is enough evidence here to conclude that Jesus and the disciples had money, enough that they needed a financial manager—a treasurer.

Now, if it was ok for Jesus and his disciples to have money, we can conclude that it is ok for us to have money. It was not a sin for Jesus and the disciples to be wealthy. Indeed, it was necessary for the furtherance of Jesus' ministry.

KING'S KIDS

The Bible tells us we are sons and daughters of the Most High King. That makes us royalty.

> *But you are a chosen people, a royal priesthood, a holy nation, a people belonging to God, that you may declare the praises of him who called you out of darkness into his wonderful light.*

1 Peter 2:9 NIV

Most king's kids are wealthy. They are princes and princesses. They have money. Look at the royalty of England. You ever see Prince Charles pull up in a rusted-out 1972 Pinto? No. He rides in a Rolls Royce. Why? Because royalty has wealth, especially when you have your own country.

To Make Wealth

Lest there be any doubt concerning God's heart regarding wealth, consider Moses' words to the children of Israel during the time that they were being reestablished with the Father God:

> *But remember the Lord your God, for it is he who gives you the ability to produce wealth, and so confirms his covenant, which he swore to your ancestors, as it is today.*

> Deuteronomy 8:18 NIV

If God wanted us poor, why would he give us the ability to produce wealth? Notice also that this is a covenant that he swore to our ancestors *as it is today*. That means it applies *today*...tomorrow and every day. We have a sworn covenant from God Almighty declaring our ability to produce wealth. God does not go back on his sworn covenants. His word is true, never changing. So today, we have the ability to earn wealth and be wealthy. Tomorrow, the same.

Summary

Maybe you are struggling to make ends meet; statistics show that most people are. Or maybe you are one of the few with the opposite problem: What do to with all your money? Regardless of whether you are broke or wealthy, please stay with me. This is not a get-rich-quick plan. Rather, it is a study of God's heart for his people and the simple steps it takes to reach his highest for our lives.

God's blessings are offered universally, but they are given individually. Some of us are called to great wealth. Others are called to moderate wealth. Some will be called into areas where they are dependent on the wealth of others. The key is in knowing

God's calling for your life and walking in it. Make no mistake, however, wealth is an essential part of the Kingdom of God and the lives of his children.

That is why it is God's will for his people to create wealth—to have an abundance to be able to meet our needs and the needs of others and to enjoy the material blessings of his love.

I hope you can accept this truth. If you still struggle, thinking it is wrong to have an abundance of financial resources, or if you now realize you have made money mammon, the god of money, I suggest you repent before God and ask for forgiveness. Ask the Lord to change your perspective about wealth and to impart his view of it for your life.

4

Mountain Climbing

IMAGINE A MOUNTAIN representing the world's businesses and economies. At its base would be the poorest person in the world, and at the top, the richest person in the world (right below Jeff Bezos, the founder of Amazon, of course). Everyone else fits somewhere in between.

To advance the Kingdom of God through society, God wants us to move up the mountain. He wants us to obtain higher levels and to exert godly influence in the realms of business and finance.

This premise is based on the concept of seven mountains that control or influence everything in society. The mountains are family, religion, education, government, media, arts & entertainment, business & economy. There are a few variations in the classification of the mountains, but the one I want to explore is the mountain of business and economy.

FROM THEIR NEIGHBORS

The Bible talks about transferring wealth from the ungodly to the godly. We see an example of this when the Israelites fled Egypt for their desert rendezvous with God's destiny.

> *Now the children of Israel had done according to the word of Moses, and they had asked from the Egyptians articles of silver, articles of gold, and clothing. And the Lord had given the people favor in the sight of the Egyptians, so that they granted*

25

them what they requested. Thus, they plundered the Egyptians.

Exodus 12:35-36

The Israelites were slaves in Egypt. They had nothing. They owned nothing. They were the poorest of the poor. But when God led them out of captivity, they left laden with gold and silver. There was a transfer of wealth from the ungodly Egyptians to God's chosen people.

Lacking any experience in managing wealth, especially the windfall they acquired just before they left, the Israelites made some mistakes along the way. The Bible tells us they melted some of the gold to form a calf to worship in the desert. While this displeased God (to say the least) there is an underlying point here.

It's unlikely this calf was the size of a thimble. More likely, it was a full-size calf weighing hundreds of pounds. Imagine the amount of gold this required, and the significant sum this represented in their economy at the time. Clearly, the Israelites, God's chosen people, were wealthy. Unfortunately, they chose to worship it.

Contributing to their prosperity is the fact that their needs were few. The Bible tells us their clothes and sandals never wore out for 40 years. (Went out of style, yes, but never wore out.) Further, God supplied their food and drink. Manna fell from heaven and water flowed from rocks. Thus, they were able to save their wealth on this all-expense-paid journey through the Sinai.

UNGODLY TO GODLY

Let's look at other scriptures that illustrate the transfer of wealth.

26

> *To the person who pleases him, God gives wisdom, knowledge and happiness, but <u>to the sinner he gives the task of gathering and storing up wealth to hand it over to the one who pleases God.</u>*

Ecclesiastes 2:26 NIV (emphasis added)

Because the wealth of the ungodly is being transferred to the godly, it stands to reason that the unrighteous have the task of acquiring wealth for the righteous. No matter how we slice it, they are storing up wealth to hand over to those who please God, and this includes Christians.

> *A good person leaves an inheritance for their children's children, but a sinner's wealth is stored up for the righteous.*

Proverbs 13:22 NIV

It doesn't get much clearer. The sinner, unrighteous and ungodly is storing up wealth to hand over to Christians, to the righteous and godly. So, if God wanted us poor as a path to holiness, why does he keep trying to give us other people's wealth?

Notice something else about this scripture. "A good person leaves an inheritance to their children's children." Think about it. It takes a fair amount of money to leave something for both your children *and* your grandchildren. This is obviously talking about a person of great wealth...and that person is called "good."

TRANSFER OF INFLUENCE

The mountain of business and economy has always existed. It is full of gold, silver, finances, power—in a word: *wealth*. In these modern times, the unrighteous rule the mountain. The body of Christ vacated the mountain, believing poverty was godly. Worse, a few of us went to the other extreme and started worshiping money (mammon).

Today, we are looking for more than money. Yes, scripture promises the transfer of wealth from ungodly hands to godly hands. But a more accurate understanding of God's mandate is the transfer of *influence* on the mountain.

You see, the wealth doesn't move. It remains on the mountain. That's why it's called the mountain of business and economy. It is we who move—those in power, the influencers. It is time for the godly to move back onto the mountain and the ungodly to move off the mountain.

Of course, it is not the extreme top of the mountain that most of us should seek. That is a narrow slot, reserved for a select few. Rather, it is the places in between that we will inhabit. Certainly, there are a few believers near the top of the mountain. The problem is there are too many non-believers there as well. Their wealth needs to be transferred to the believers.

Why do we need to be striving toward the top at all? Why can't we be content with being a little further up the mountain? The reason is more than wealth. It is position, power and influence. Under the oppressive poverty spirit, we made our camp at the bottom. Christians, however, are filled with the Spirit of God. It is time we start climbing the mountain with one goal in mind: the furtherance of the Kingdom of God.

Robert Henderson put it well.

> *When the wicked lose their wealth, they lose their influence and power. When Christians receive wealth, we gain influence and power.*

I am sure you have heard of these wealthy people and their opinions: Rosie O'Donnell, Mark Cuban, Michael Moore, Oprah Winfrey, and Donald Trump. (Please note, I am neither condemning nor condoning what they represent, only using them as examples of wealthy people who are highly influential.) Can you appreciate the fact that because they have money, they have a platform from which they influence our politics and morals?

One even became President in 2014. I remember 30 years ago a news program was interviewing some guy who was building skyscrapers and casinos. In fact, he was frequently on the news. That's how most people had heard of Donald Trump prior to his run for the presidency. His views on issues other than real estate were well known, as he is quite vocal. Interestingly, at that time, he influenced people because he was a wealthy businessperson. His decisions were shaping society. Therefore, the news media wanted to know his thoughts.

Now, if Trump had been a janitor at one of the skyscrapers he was building, would he have been interviewed? Not likely. But because he had wealth, lots of it, he had the media's attention.

What if our major Christian leaders were also billionaires and had the influence on society of, say, Oprah Winfrey? Leaders like:

- Jon Benefiel (founder, Heartland Apostolic Prayer Network)
- Bill Johnson (founder of Bethel Church)
- Rick Warren (founder of Saddle Back Church)
- Faisal Malick (founder of Plumb Line Ministries)

Could you imagine the impact on society? Picture the news media asking them about the direction our country should take on issues such as abortion, marijuana, healthcare or government. Their influence, combined with our influence, would change our culture, the country and the world. We could be a planet that stands for God.

I get excited just thinking of the possibilities.

FIVE KEYS TO MAKING WEALTH

We must get to the top of that mountain. To that end, God has shown me five keys to making and managing wealth. The first one, stewardship, is so important that I have broken it down into three subkeys.

1. Stewardship
    a. Who Owns It?
    b. Who's the Provider?
    c. Stewards
2. Tithe
3. Give
4. Spend
5. Thankfulness

In the next several chapters, I will show you what I have learned and what I practice in my own life. These principles have worked for me, and I believe they will work for you.

5

My World On Fire

THE YEAR WAS 1988. The previous year, I had been offered a chance to buy my father's business—*Thermocel*. It manufactured exothermic powders for the steel industry. I partnered with the salesman, Bill. The plan was that on January 1, 1988, Bill and I would each own a third of the business.

My Grandfather started the company in 1948. My dad came to work for him in the early 1950s. My grandfather passed away soon afterward, so my dad ran the company on his own from then until 1987. I started working there as a laborer at age 16. Dad had been ready to retire for a few years, so he had not focused much on expanding the business. I saw room for improvement.

In 1986, representatives of another company came to see the shop with the intent to buy it. I happen to be on break when they came through the breakroom on a tour of the facility. Dad was called to take a phone call and asked me to talk with the potential new owners. I spent a few minutes with them until he returned, then I went back to my job. At this time, I was a foreman—basically a laborer who did most of the maintenance.

That evening, my wife and I went to my parents for dinner. While there, Dad asked, "What did you tell them when I was taking the phone call today?"

"I told them about the flow of the shop and the maintenance," I answered.

"Well, you must have impressed them. If they make an offer, it will be contingent on you staying and running the company for them," said Dad.

The company eventually backed out of the deal, but it opened Dad's eyes to my ability to run it. He asked if I had any interest in buying the company. Yes, I said, but I did not want to do sales. I wanted to manage production and purchasing. At the time, Dad did sales. So, we hired Bill to be our salesman, the person who would eventually buy a third of the company with me. Bill was a great salesman and started getting new customers. Soon, we were busier than ever.

Meanwhile, I began making changes to improve production. Since I had worked in the factory for many years, I had ideas about how to make things run more efficiently. By the time I was done making changes, production ran like a well-oiled machine. Bill was bringing in lots of new work and I was turning it out in record time. We were a great team.

Bill and I made a deal with a handshake to each buy a third of the company on January 1, 1988. Although no deal had been signed for buying the company, Bill and I were now partners with Dad.

One morning in late May, I arrived early to load my truck with a pallet of product and take it to a steel mill where Bill would meet me. I was ready to go when it happened.

An employee came running up yelling "Fire, Fire!"

BURN THE STAGE

I quickly ran through the building to the area where he reported the fire. I remember thinking: It's probably nothing, as this guy tends to exaggerate things. But as I rounded the corner, I saw several empty fire extinguishers on the ground and a fire 20 feet wide and blazing up to the ceiling.

We were in trouble.

The building was constructed of block walls and wooden trusses, with wood decking and shingles. It was built in 1890, so the wood was nearly one hundred years old. Aged wood burns exceedingly well. Making things worse, our product, exothermic powders, burns on its own at about 3,000 deg. F.

Now, for a fire to burn, it needs three things—a heat source (ignition), fuel and oxygen. For fuel, there were paper bags, wood pallets, the wood structure of the building itself, and more importantly, barrels of aluminum powder which is part of the exothermic reaction. For oxygen, there was air, but there were also barrels of Sodium Chlorate, a chemical that actually generates oxygen when it burns. The combination of the aluminum powder with sodium chlorate makes a fantastic exothermic reaction.

We had the settings for a perfect fire.

ASHES TO ASHES

The fire was quickly spreading. I sent someone to call the fire department. Fortunately, they were right next door. Unfortunately, this was a small-town volunteer fire department. As seconds turned to hours, the fire department finally arrived, but it was two men in a pick-up truck. They had actually driven past the property and finally came in from the backside.

Clarence was the fire chief. He was nearly 80 years old. When he saw the raging fire, which was now consuming most of our production area and blazing thirty feet above the roofline, he screamed:

"Bob, that fire's too big for us."

He radioed in for help. We finally ended up with five fire departments and over eighty firemen. They put out the flames and that was it.

(see finishlineresources.com for pictures of the fire)

After ensuring that all of my workers were safe, I got busy helping the fire department and giving interviews to several local TV stations and newspapers. My wife, Laurie, heard about the fire and rushed to the scene. She was five months pregnant with our first daughter and was worried about me. I assured her I was OK and that I had to continue helping with the fire.

The six hours it took to get the fire put out flew by like minutes but seemed like days. As things calmed down, I wandered away from the burned down building to a separate building that had not burned. It was on a hill above the smoldering ruins of our main building. From my vantage point, I could see that we had lost all of our production area. The roof was gone, so was every wire, bearing, motor, seal, rubber elevator belt...incinerated. All that was left was the block walls and the steel hulks of the charred machines. Our factory was gone and my future with it.

I became enraged, screaming: "God, how could you do this to me?!"

At that moment, God answered me in the most audible voice I have ever heard him speak. It felt like everyone for miles could hear God's stern voice: "I give the blessing, and I can take it away!"

I was reduced to ashes.

6

Stewardship—Who Owns It?

IT IS GOD'S WILL FOR HIS SONS AND DAUGHTERS to create wealth, to receive the transfer of wealth from the ungodly to godly, and to rise in influence on the mountain of business and economics.

Let's explore how to handle wealth—a problem I want each of my readers to have. As Christians, we need a godly perspective of wealth. This starts with an understanding of stewardship.

Stewardship, definition: "The conducting, supervising, or managing of something; especially: the careful and responsible management of something entrusted to one's care."

If something is entrusted to our care, it means someone else owns it. If I am entrusted with the maintenance of a home, it means an owner has charged me to take care of it.

So, when it comes to wealth, who owns it? Is it ours? Do we own it?

Strange as it may sound, we don't own anything. I know... I said we were created to make wealth, and I even backed it up with scriptures. It's true. We are created for wealth, but we don't own anything. As you read through the next few chapters, this will make sense.

So, who owns our wealth—our money, houses, cars and cool stuff? Let's look at Psalms.

The earth is the Lord's, and everything in it, the world, and all who live in it.

Psalm 24:1 NIV

God is saying he owns the world, everything in it and all who live here. What is left for us to own?

Let's look at Haggai:

> *"The silver is mine and the gold is mine," declares the Lord Almighty.*

Haggai 2:8 NIV

The silver and gold are his? Don't silver and gold represent currency to us? At one point in the United States of America, our currency was backed by gold. So, God is telling us our money is his.

David goes a step further:

> *Yours, O Lord, is the greatness and the power and the glory and majesty and the splendor, for everything in heaven and earth is yours.*

1 Chronicles 29:11 NIV

David declares that everything in heaven and earth is the Lord's. Not just material wealth, but everything—power, glory, majesty and splendor. Beginning to get the picture? We don't own a thing. Nothing, nada, zilch, diddly-squat. Everything in heaven and earth is the Lord's, including...heaven and earth!

NET WORTH

Have you ever been asked your net worth? Perhaps when you applied for a loan, the application had you list your assets such as your house, cars, land—anything that has a resale value. Then they had you list the liabilities such as a mortgage, car payment and credit card debt. When you subtract your liabilities from your assets, you get your net worth.

Perhaps you have paid off some of your home. Maybe you own your cars. You might have a net worth of $75,000 according to the bank. But scripture says our net worth is $0 since we don't own anything. God owns it all. You are the steward of $75,000, but you are not the owner of it. We will talk about this more in the chapters to come.

By the way, if you apply for a loan, they will assume you are the owner. Don't argue with them, because you won't get the loan without some assets. Afterward, however, feel free to leave them a copy of my book.

WALK LIKE A CAMEL

Remember the scripture comparing a rich man to a camel?

Again I tell you, it is easier for a camel to go through the eye of a needle than for someone who is rich to enter the kingdom of God.

Matthew 19:24 NIV

I have wrestled with this scripture; many people I know wrestle with it too. The prevailing teaching is that the eye of the needle was a gate that camels had to crawl through to enter the city after dark. Well, I did some research and discovered that this theory came about hundreds of years after the verse was written. Historians cannot find any evidence of a gate called "the eye of the needle." I think we are misunderstanding this scripture.

Here's my understanding of the passage.

If God owns everything, including all my money and stuff, then I own nothing. Therefore, I am not rich and I can get into heaven.

Understanding this was very freeing to me since God had blessed my wife and me with a nice house, newer cars and a fair amount of stuff. With this understanding, I no longer needed to struggle with whether I was rich, or how rich, or even how to define *rich*. I didn't have to worry whether it would be hard for me to enter the Kingdom of God. It is no problem, as I have no net worth. I am merely a steward of God's stuff. Entering heaven as a rich man is not a problem I have, because I'm not a rich man. I'm a steward of a rich man—God.

LOVE AND THEFT

Consider this scenario. If I, a stranger, took your car without permission, you would call the police and tell them your car was stolen. Now, because I stole your car, that makes me a thief because I took ownership of what belonged to you.

In essence, haven't we become thieves by taking ownership of what belongs to God?

Now, if I stole your car, I would need to give it back (with a full tank of gas, of course) and ask your forgiveness, right? Well, we need to repent and ask forgiveness for taking ownership of what belongs to God. And we need to give ownership back to the owner—the Lord God Almighty, the rightful owner.

Please take a minute and ask God to forgive you for taking ownership of what doesn't belong to you. In the process, give it all back to him. After repenting, let God change your perspective about ownership. Learn to constantly remind yourself, "It's not mine! It's Gods!"

Build reminders into your daily life. Post the scriptures we listed on your bathroom mirror, on the refrigerator door, on your car's dashboard. For me, the more I see or think about God owning things, the easier it is for me to live with that mindset.

Make it a goal to change your perspective to "Everything is God's."

Do it before everything burns to the ground.

7

Magnificent Defeat

THE FIRE OF 1988 TOOK nearly everything I knew and loved. At least, that is how it felt. Hearing God's rebuke: "I give the blessing and I can take it away," was a purging fire that destroyed my self-styled ambition.

I was a young man of 27 who had just made a fifty-year-old company run better than it ever had. I was proud of it, yet I was taking credit for being the provider, the one who made this business succeed. In reality, it was God who provided. It was his responsibility, not mine. I was just a youth who didn't know who the provider was...yet. When God spoke those words to me, I quickly repented for my wrong attitude of ownership.

In the months that followed my surrender, a new plan was coming to fruition. In the end, one of the worst events of my life became one of the best events of my life.

Dad, Bill and I decided to rebuild the shop. In the ensuing days, I called all the employees together and laid out a plan to clean up the mess, tear apart all the equipment and work out a plan to rebuild or replace it. Dad designed a new roof and secured a builder. We found an electrician for the rewiring of everything. With everyone now engaged, I occupied myself with tearing apart 30 gear reducers. I ordered motors and seals for all of them. To everyone's amazement, we were back up and operating in 10 days. All we lacked was a roof, but hey, roofs are overrated anyway.

By August, we had our roof. Remarkably, in the two and a half months it took to construct it, we only lost half a day's production due to rain. You see, 1988 was a drought year in Ohio. For farmers, this was a disaster but for us, it was a blessing. Because our finished-goods warehouse did not burn down, we had enough stock to ensure that we never missed an order.

We now had a better building with modern lighting, insulation, restored equipment and a new approach to ownership. Our customers admired our grit and respected us for staying in business to serve their needs. God turned a financial disaster into a financial opportunity by first adjusting my thinking.

He is the provider, not me.

AFTERMATH

Looking back on the event, I realized that I had sinned in my approach to creating wealth. However, I had done so out of ignorance. In the months that followed the fire, as God and I sifted through the ashes of my convicted heart, I found comfort in the scriptures regarding anyone who sins unintentionally. From Leviticus:

> *The Lord said to Moses, "Say to the Israelites: 'When anyone sins unintentionally and does what is forbidden in any of the Lord's commands—if the anointed priest sins, bringing guilt on the people, he must bring to the Lord a young bull without defect as a sin offering for the sin he has committed.'*

> *'In this way the priest will make atonement for them for the sin they have committed, and they will be forgiven.'"*

> Leviticus 4:1-3, 35 NIV

When we take ownership as the provider, we have sinned. But it is an unintentional sin. For me, I never got in God's face and said, "I am taking ownership and I am the provider!" Rather, it was a role I assumed, one that was taught by society. My error was unintentional. Yes, it was wrong and sinful and not what God intended, but it was recoverable through my contrite heart.

Today, whenever I think I am doing something great by my own ability, I think back to the fire and remember that I am nothing without God. I hope you can learn the same without going through what I went through—a fiery loss of all I'd worked for.

REPENTANCE

Let us consider repenting for trying to be the provider. If we have taken on a role that is not ours to have, we need to ask forgiveness for taking the position that we are the provider when scripture clearly shows God is the provider.

Will you take a minute and repent and pray for forgiveness?

May God forgive you, heal you and prosper you in accordance with his word.

8

Stewardship—Who's the Provider?

WHEN MY SECOND DAUGHTER was a young teenager, she nicknamed me NBOD. If you're a dad, you are, or will become, the NBOD, "National Bank Of Dad."

Does any of this sound familiar?

- Dad, I need money to go to the movies.
- Dad, my friends and I are going to the mall; I need some money.
- Dad, we are going out to eat; I need some cash.
- Dad, I need a prom dress.
- Dad, I need a homecoming dress.
- Dad, I need a new outfit.
- Dad, I need school clothes.

(Can you tell I had all daughters?)

Our children come to us and ask us to provide for their needs. My daughter thought I was the provider. But as I look at scripture, I find I am mistaken in being the provider.

Let's start with Luke:

> *Consider the ravens: They do not sow or reap; they have no storeroom or barn; yet God feeds them. And how much more valuable you are than birds.*
>
> Luke 12:24 NIV

Interestingly, God is talking about ravens, blackbirds and crows—the least valuable of birds. Have you ever gone to a pet shop and seen crows for sale? You might see parrots, cockatiels, finches and other exotic birds, but you won't find blackbirds unless they're singing in the dead of night. They're not rare; in fact, they're plentiful. Here in Ohio, the farmers hate them because they devour their crops. Yet God used a nearly worthless bird to say that just as he provides for them, he will provide for us.

He goes on to say how much more valuable we are than birds. We are valuable to God. I like that. He treasures us. He loves us. So, if God supplies for the crows and he values us even more, doesn't it make sense that he will provide for us as well?

In the next verse it says:

> *Who of you by worrying (stressing) can add a single hour to your life?*

> Luke 12:25 NIV

"Who of you...can add...?" The correct answer is "No one."

By some estimates, stress causes 85% of all illnesses. It ruins our immune system. In particular, stressing over our money can actually make us sick. Stress is hard on the body and wears it out, so not only does stress not add an hour to your life, it shortens your life.

God, in his infinite wisdom, knows that if we let him provide for us and we don't worry about it, we will live longer healthier lives.

> *Abraham looked up and there in a thicket he saw a ram caught by its horns. He went over and took the ram and sacrificed it as a burnt offering instead of*

46

*his son. So Abraham called that place The Lord Will
Provide. And to this day it is said, "On the mountain
of the Lord it will be provided."*

Genesis 22:13-14 NIV

In this passage, the name used for God is *Jehovah-Jireh*,
meaning "The Lord will provide!" This is one of the many names
of God. His name proclaims that he will provide for us! Notice the
word *will*. It doesn't say *might, sometimes* or if he *feels like it*. This
is a proclamation. he *will* provide.

OUR WANTS AND NEEDS

The Apostle Paul wrote the definitive word on God's
provision in his letter to the Philippians.

*And my God will meet all your needs according to
the riches of his glory in Christ Jesus.*

Philippians 4:19 NIV

This verse makes an interesting distinction, however. Notice
the three-letter word *all*. It doesn't say *some* of our needs, or
when God *feels like it*, or on a *good day*, or when you *walk
perfectly*. It simply says, "God will meet *all* your needs."

Notice the word *needs*. People, especially Americans, seem
to think everything they want is a need. They need the biggest,
newest TV. Or they need a new car because theirs is three years
old. *Hey, the new model gets a mile more per gallon.* Or they need
a pool because the neighbors all have pools and they must make
a splash.

Newsflash: These are not *needs*. These are *wants*. There is a
difference. Needs are the things we must have to survive. Wants
are the extras, the luxuries, stuff we would like to have.

Now, please understand, I am not saying God wants us to live in poverty with only the basic needs provided—food, water, shelter and high-speed internet. I am saying that we have misinterpreted what our needs are.

God is a father. Speaking as a father, I love to give my children gifts. I love to give them what they need to survive, but I also love to give them the gifts they desire. When my girls were growing up, my wife and I gave them food every day, clothes to wear to school, but we also gave them things they wanted: dolls, play kitchens, bikes, MP3 players, video games, books and other things. It was a great joy to give them things that they didn't need but wanted. Sometimes, our girls had to wait a while, until Christmas or their birthday, but we wanted to bless them and give them more than just their needs.

God works the same way. He provides our basic needs, but he loves to lavish us with gifts. Yet some of us can't wait for God to gift us with our desires, so we borrow the money and buy them now. Then we find ourselves burdened with credit card debt and loan payments and we start stressing over our finances, shortening our lives with worry, failing in our occupations and lessening our ability to make wealth in the first place.

This is not at all what God wants for us. Since he is the owner of everything, he is the only one who can provide anything.

RICH MAN POOR MAN

> *Command those who are rich in this present world*
> *not to be arrogant nor to put their hope in wealth,*
> *which is so uncertain, but to put their hope in God,*

> *who richly provides us with everything for our enjoyment.*

> 1 Timothy 6:17 NIV

This is a great scripture. For starters, "put their hope in God, who richly provides us with everything," sums things up beautifully. God is our provider.

Furthermore, the scripture says nothing negative about having wealth. It just says we need the right perspective about it: "those who are rich in this present world not to be arrogant nor put their hope in wealth." It is ok to have wealth, just don't be arrogant about it. Those who are wealthy are no more important than those in poverty.

Poverty is a temporary state of lack, a place from which to reach up and reach out, to seek God for your needs and your wants. It is a time to evaluate the roots of your condition with the understanding that it is not God's will for his children to suffer lack.

When God looks at us, he does not see how much money we have. He sees our hearts. If a heart is arrogant, possessed of the wrong attitudes about wealth, he sees that and deals with it.

We need God's perspective.

When you see someone wealthy, do you think they are better than you? Do you become envious? This is an important consideration, for jealousy and envy are subtle forms of money-worship.

It is wrong to rank a person based on their wealth. God does not view us that way, nor should we. Let us value people for who they are, not what they have or what we think they can give us. How many times have we put our hope in wealth, thinking that if we had more money, everything would be better? This is a false hope; it is trusting in a lie. God is our hope. All good things flow from him. He is our provider, our hope for the future. And as I found out through the factory fire, you can be wealthy one minute and broke the next. Our riches are in God.

WANT IT NOW!

Here is a question: When we are impatient for something we want (not need), and we take out a loan for it, do we deprive God of the privilege of blessing us? Let me give you an example.

I know several people who have been given new (or nearly new) cars as a gift—no payments. At times, these have been given anonymously, and the people who received these generous gifts were totally blessed and amazed at the generous gift of God through the heart of a believer.

Now, turn it around. What if they had gone out the week before, borrowed money and bought a nice car? They would have missed God's provision and blessing.

I think we are impatient at times, with a "want it now" mentality instead of waiting on God. Maybe we need to stop and ask God what he wants us to do—borrow or wait for him to provide. Certainly, there are times when we are to borrow and other times not borrow. That is something God needs to speak about to each of us.

What would our lives look like if we allowed God to provide? If we waited on him to bless us? Would life be less stressful? Would we be more focused on God and less focused on our financial circumstances? I think so, and scripture bears this out.

But those who wait on the Lord
Shall renew their strength;
They shall mount up with wings like eagles,
They shall run and not be weary,
They shall walk and not faint.

Isaiah 40:31

BRING HOME THE BACON

I would like to address the misconception: "Men are the providers." When I was growing up, my dad taught me through his actions that the man is the provider for the family. He goes to work to earn money so he can provide for the family. That was my dad's contribution to the family. My mom's responsibility was to raise my sisters and me.

Many of us have been instilled with similar values. Although it sent a generation of men to work each day and brought them home at night, it is not entirely scriptural. Somewhere in our evolution as a society, we wandered from the truth of God as the provider. Yes, it is our responsibility to work, but it is God's responsibility to provide for all.

Wealth and honor come from you [God].

1 Chronicles 29:12 NIV (emphasis added)

Men, we cannot make wealth on our own. It comes from God. He, and only he, can give it. Recall from the last chapter that God owns everything including wealth. So only he can provide it.

51

9

Stewardship and Stewards

IF YOU BEEN AROUND CHURCH for very long, you have heard many sermons on stewardship. But what exactly does stewardship mean?

Stewardship, definition: "the conducting, supervising, or managing of something; especially: the careful and responsible management of something entrusted to one's care."

From this definition, stewardship is precisely what Christians are called to do with their lives. Let's look at what the Bible says about stewardship.

> *So God created mankind in his own image, in the image of God he created them; male and female he created them.*
>
> *God blessed them and said to them, "Be fruitful and increase in number; fill the earth and subdue it. Rule over the fish in the sea and the birds in the sky and over every living creature that moves on the ground."*
>
> *The Lord God took the man and put him in the Garden of Eden to work and take care of it.*
>
> Genesis 1:27-28, 2:15 NIV

God put Adam and Eve in the garden to work and care for it. The Bible doesn't say he gave them the garden as their possession. It speaks of Adam and Eve filling the earth and subduing it. This was a major task, not to be undertaken alone.

Remember, the definition of stewardship includes, "Responsible management of something entrusted to one's care." And we know from earlier studies that "the earth is the Lord's and everything in it" (Psalm 24:1). Hence, Adam and Eve were the first stewards of the garden and the earth at large.

Taking care of the garden had to be an awesome job, however. Think about it. They didn't have to water the garden. "A river watering the garden flowed from Eden..." (Genesis 2:10 NIV). And they didn't have to plant anything, because God already did that. "Now the Lord God had planted a garden in the east, in Eden" (Genesis 2:8 NIV). So, what did they have to do to work and care for the garden? I can only think of two things—prune the branches and harvest the food. Sweet deal!

JESUS AS STEWARD

Jesus was also a steward of the Father. He was entrusted with his physical body and he managed it for the Father's purpose. Our salvation comes from Jesus' stewardship. Jesus gave his life because his life was not his own but was entrusted to him from God. He managed it according to what the owner, Father God, wanted. It wasn't always easy.

> Going a little farther, he [Jesus] fell with his face to the ground and prayed, "My father, if it is possible, may this cup be taken from me. Yet not as I will, but as you will."

Matthew 26:39 NIV (emphasis added)

Have you ever heard the phrase, "I gave my life to the Lord"? It is a common thing to hear at altar calls. "Come forward if you would like to give your life to the Lord."

Well, if we give our lives to the Lord, we no longer own our lives, right? So, we must be managing what has been entrusted to us. By definition, when we become Christians, we begin stewardship of our lives. As we grow in Christ, as he forms his likeness within us, the question then becomes: "How good of a steward are you?"

A GOOD STEWARD

Let's look at a famous passage on stewardship: Matthew 25:14-30. It is commonly referred to as the Parable of the Talents. God has given me some gems about this passage that I'd love to share with you. Let's start at verse 14:

> *Again, it will be like a man going on a journey, who called his servants and entrusted his wealth to them.*

> Matthew 25:14 NIV

Notice the word *entrusted*. It sounds like the definition of stewardship: "the responsible management of something *entrusted* to one's care." In this parable, the master made his servants into stewards by entrusting them with a portion of his wealth.

> *To one he gave five bags of gold, to another two bags, and to another one bag, each according to his ability. Then he went on his journey.*

> Matthew 25:15 NIV

Consider the phrase, "each according to his own ability." Earlier we read that God gives us the ability to produce wealth. These three servants had probably proven themselves able to do the same. The master did not find random strangers and entrust his wealth to them. No, these were people he knew and trusted with his talents.

Have you ever wondered how much money a talent is? I did some research and found a talent equaled 20 years of a laborer's wage. I looked up the current laborer's wage and found many different numbers, so I averaged them. I used $30,000 per year and multiplied that by 20 years. I was astounded to find that each talent equaled $600,000. That was some serious coin. This chart shows the full value entrusted to each servant.

Number of Talents	Talent 20 years	Talent value	Total value
5	20	$30,000	$3,000,000
3	20	$30,000	$1,200,000
1	20	$30,000	$600,000
		Total	$4,800,000

That's a total of $4,800,000! This master was pretty well off and he entrusted a lot to his servants. As I said before, I doubt these were random men he found on the street and said, "Hey, you! Here's $4,800,000 Do something with it." This rich master probably had lots of servants, and it's safe to assume that some of his servants managed his money for him. They watched over his investments, made recommendations for investments and had been proven worthy of the task.

Let's read the remaining passage.

The man who had received five bags of gold went at once and put his money to work and gained five bags more. So also, the one with two bags of gold gained two more. But the man who had received one bag went off, dug a hole in the ground and hid his master's money.

"After a long time the master of those servants returned and settled accounts with them. The man who had received five bags of gold brought the other five. 'Master,' he said, 'you entrusted me with five bags of gold. See, I have gained five more.'

"His master replied, 'Well done, good and faithful servant! You have been faithful with a few things; I will put you in charge of many things. Come and share your master's happiness!'

"The man with two bags of gold also came. 'Master,' he said, 'you entrusted me with two bags of gold; see, I have gained two more.'

"His master replied, 'Well done, good and faithful servant! You have been faithful with a few things; I will put you in charge of many things. Come and share your master's happiness!'

"Then the man who had received one bag of gold came. 'Master,' he said, 'I knew that you are a hard man, harvesting where you have not sown and gathering where you have not scattered seed. So I was afraid and went out and hid your gold in the ground. See, here is what belongs to you.'

"His master replied, 'You wicked, lazy servant! So you knew that I harvest where I have not sown and gather where I have not scattered seed? Well then, you should have put my money on deposit with the bankers, so that when I returned I would have received it back with interest.

"'So take the bag of gold from him and give it to the one who has ten bags. For whoever has will be given more, and they will have an abundance. Whoever does not have, even what they have will be taken from them. And throw that worthless servant outside, into the darkness, where there will be weeping and gnashing of teeth.'

Matthew 25:16-30 NIV

First, the obvious. All three stewards knew what the master wanted— a gain on his money, commonly called ROI (Return On Investment). The third one even said he knew the master was a hard man who harvested where he did not sow. So, they all knew what was expected of them.

Yet there were two types of stewards. The two stewards with five talents and two talents respectively were called *good stewards*. Then you have the guy with one talent, who was called *lazy, wicked* and *worthless*. That's a bit harsh, isn't it? Maybe he had issues. Perhaps he was absent the day they taught ROI. It's even questionable if he was a steward at all since by definition, a steward exercises "careful and responsible management of something entrusted to one's care." He was neither careful nor responsible. But we will be kind and call him the *not-so-good steward*.

Now, some people read this scripture and see two masters—a nice guy and a horrible guy, based on how he treats his servants. He even comes across as a bit schizophrenic, loving some but castigating others. The key, however, is in the perspective.

Notice how these stewards viewed the master. The good stewards knew him as generous and loving. The NIV quotes him as saying to them, "Come and share in your master's happiness."

What does that look like? I would imagine the master was extremely happy with the ROI from these servants. He just made $3,000,000; why shouldn't he be happy?

If I gave you $3,000,000 to invest, and when I came back, you returned $6,000,000, I would be ecstatic. You just doubled my money! I can guarantee, I would not walk calmly up to you, shake your hand and hand you a $50 Outback Gift Card. No way! We would be celebrating. My wife and I would be taking you and your spouse on a first-class, all-expense-paid vacation to Hawaii. I would not nitpick anything you did to double the money (as long as I didn't need a lawyer). I might ask how you did it in general, but overall, I'd be excited for your success...for our success.

You, in turn, would see me as a good boss, supportive and excited for your reward. That's how the good stewards saw their master.

Now, the not-so-good steward knew the master as hard and demanding. Let's look at our example again.

If I gave you $600,000 to invest, and when I came back, you handed me $600,000, I would ask, "Where's the money you made?"

If you said, "I hid it in the ground. I didn't even take it to the bank for interest," I would be furious! I might even lose my temper.

"What do you mean, you hid it in the ground! You idiot! You're fired!"

At that moment, wouldn't your perspective of me be different than the person who just doubled my money? To you, I am a hard man, reaping where I did not sow. To the others, I'm Father Christmas. To you, I'm the Grinch. Yet, I am one in the same in this example, both supportive and excited but also demanding and hard. Same person, two different perspectives.

So, I would ask, what is your perspective of the master in this story? Is he kind and generous or hard and demanding?

We just looked at how the servants knew the master. Now let us look at their rewards. Both the good stewards and not-so-good steward received rewards. The good stewards were each praised. "Well done good and faithful servant." But the not-so-good steward was denigrated as "wicked and lazy." Not the reward I would want. What about you?

The good stewards were rewarded with generosity and given greater responsibility. But the not-so-good steward was rewarded with poverty, losing what little he had to begin with.

Finally, the good stewards were rewarded with joy. "Come and share in your master's happiness." The not-so-good steward was rewarded with misery, expulsion and "weeping and gnashing of teeth."

So, the same master, but two totally different perspectives based on the quality of the stewards. Each of the stewards brought out a different side to the same master's personality.

How do you see God? Is he the good master when it comes to wealth? Or is he the hard master? The difference could be in your attitude toward wealth.

MY FATHER SIDE

I have three daughters, all on their own now. Growing up, they mostly knew me as fun, playful and pleasant. But occasionally, they saw me in a different light. When they crossed the line, broke a rule or otherwise disobeyed me, I became the disciplinarian. My girls did not like it when Dad had to discipline them. They hated it. In fact, I am sure at times they hated me. Now, I tried to be fair in all discipline, but there were times when my girls needed discipline. They had just one dad, me. The guy who could be loving and playful could also be harsh and punishing. Same Dad, different perspectives.

The perspective my girls had of me was based on their actions and attitudes. If they were disobedient, a different side came out of me, thus their perspective of me changed. Likewise, in Matthew 25, the perspectives of the stewards were based on what they did. The good stewards did what they were entrusted to do. The not-so-good steward didn't do what he was entrusted to do. There were consequences each way—positive and negative. It was all based on the steward's actions and attitudes.

CAN'T BUDGE IT

So, what does stewardship look like? What are we supposed to do with the resources God has entrusted to us? In the context of the parable we just studied, what does the master want us to do with his money? In Matthew, he wanted an ROI from his stewards. He wanted to make money with his money. He wanted a reward for his risk—the risk of entrusting his stewards.

What does God want us to do with his money?

Most of us have been taught to be wise and thrifty with money, to account for every cent. We are told to live debt-free, carefully considering where every penny is spent. The Christian standard, as promoted in many circles today, is to live a life of strict discipline and budget. Well...

I don't believe budgeting is what godly stewardship looks like. I think that came from a religious, man-made idea of godliness. It is not what God intended.

Now, I know that for many of you, this may be a new concept, even one that is a little hard to digest. But if you will stay with me and ask God, "What do you require of me?" I believe it will completely change your view of wealth and financial management.

Certainly, budgets can be a part of your financial planning, especially if you tend to overspend. They can be a useful tool or guideline, but budgeting isn't stewardship. Budgets can easily become religious or legalistic, and they can stifle economic growth.

In the early days, I started out with a budget in an attempt to build my savings. I wasn't legalistic. I just felt I was to start saving, and it was working. Our savings reached a fair sum of money. Then God asked me if I would be willing to give it all away. I was a little hesitant. Something big like that, you want to make sure you are hearing God correctly. I mean, this is right up there with sacrifice your son, build me a boat, or go challenge the leader of the most powerful nation on earth with nothing but a shepherd's staff and a big-mouth brother.

I told Laurie what I was sensing. She is my wise counsel. Possessed of uncommon common sense, I expected her to caution me, be apprehensive or outright opposed to the idea. Her response shocked me.

"Let's do it," she said brightly.

"Do you know how much money that is?" I said, incredulous.

"I do," she said. "But we trust God, don't we?"

Well, yes, we did. So... we did.

A couple of days later, we gave away all but a dollar in our savings and a dollar in our checkbook. We had to keep one dollar to keep the accounts open. In response, God faithfully prospered our business and replenished our savings quicker than we had saved it the first time.

Reckless? Perhaps. Godly? Certainly. Worth it? Absolutely.

Now, had I been a devoted budgeter, I would not have been obedient when God asked me to give it all away. I likely would have responded, "Sure, God. But I need to budget for it first, right? Because I've got bills to pay. It's all on a program. But I'll save up and get back to you soon. Fiscal discipline and all that, right Lord?"

I have known people to get so caught up in their budgeting, ruthlessly accounting for every penny, that they fell into worshiping their money through obsessive budgeting. That is not at all what God intends in stewardship. That is making money our god—mammon.

Compare what a rigorous budgeter does with what the not-so-good steward did. They are very similar. The budgeter following the adage: "Keep all your eggs in one basket and watch that basket." It can easily become a hoarder mentality. The not-so-good steward did exactly that. He watched his master's money by burying it. No one would get to it there, he thought. And in truth, no one did. Not one thief, nor one investor.

It's God's

A godly stewardship mindset is the first part of what God wants us to understand and do with money. It is the perspective that says: "It's God's, not mine."

Do you get that? *It's God's, not mine.*

In case you missed it: IT'S GOD'S, NOT MINE.

When we have this mindset, money will never become mammon to us. Our priorities will be in the right order. God is first. Everything else comes second, third...ninety-ninth.

Maybe you are thinking this is too simple or too hard, but really, it's just right. We need to stop thinking so highly of money and start trusting God. I constantly remind myself (by reminding God) that he is the owner and it is his responsibility to provide. (He likes it when I coach him.)

Stewardship is the careful, responsible management of something entrusted into one's care. We just need to remember: God owns the wealth. It is His responsibility to provide and direct. We are to manage it as though it is God's wealth...because it is.

Constantly ask yourself: "Would God say to me right now, 'Well done, good and faithful steward?'"

Strive to become a good steward.

10

My Stewardship Story

WE'VE ESTABLISHED who the owner is—it's God! Who the provider is—it's also God!! And who the steward serves—yep, God again.

I'd now like to tell you about stewardship from the perspective of my life. Stewardship is something I've been trying to do well for over 30 years. In that time, I've learned some things that you might find useful.

From the story of the factory fire, I recounted how I worked for my dad and eventually bought my first company from him. Later, it was nearly lost in a catastrophic fire, after which God spoke to me in no uncertain terms about who the provider is. (Turns out it was God. I should have read this book!)

Now, here's the rest of the story.

THE SPEED OF NEED

In 1994, my dad passed away, and Bill (the salesman) and I were fifty-fifty partners in the business. Bill was twenty years older than I was, and from day one, he had told me our business was a dinosaur waiting to die. In his sage wisdom, he could see that the steel industry would someday find a way to function without our product (exothermic powder) and that I should be on the lookout for another business opportunity.

In April 1996, I had a 1967 Camaro that I had restored a couple of years earlier. I had stripped it down to bare bones, painted it from the ground up, and put a 400 cubic inch motor in it. It had been my mom's first new car, a Christmas gift from Dad to Mom. I had driven the car in high school and then it sat in my parent's garage for 20 years. My wife had tried to buy it for me, but my dad insisted it was his retirement project. Then, on Christmas of 1990, he finally saw the writing on the wall and gave me the rusted-out classic. I was thrilled.

It took me a year to gather the parts and six months to rebuild it. It was completed in 1992. This was the start of my favorite hobby—restoring classic cars. Fast-forward to 1996. I had shown the Camaro at some bigger car shows but it wasn't winning. This bothered me. I like to win. Second place is the first guy to lose.

Then I read an article in Hot Rod Magazine about powder coating. I thought if I powder coated the intake and painted the firewall and inner fenders body-color, maybe the car could win a bigger car show. (Powder coating is a paint-like finish that is durable, flexible and environmentally friendly. To most, it looks just like paint.)

Thus, began my quest for a powder coating shop. I drove to Youngstown Ohio, about thirty minutes from my home, to call on a powder coating shop of good reputation. The owner told me it would be six to eight weeks until he could do my parts.

Here's a characteristic of mine: If I decide to do something, I am going to doing it right now. I am impulsive, driven by the imperative of the moment. This makes me a good racer, but not always a patient restorer. This shop's schedule wouldn't work for me, especially since I only had two weeks until the next show.

So, I traveled to Akron, Ohio, about an hour away, to a small powder coating shop. This shop was a one-person operation and he was busy, so busy that he couldn't stop to talk to me. Instead, he had me follow him to the back of the shop and talk to him while he worked. I watched as powder came out of a spray gun in a soft cloud and clung to the metal parts. Then a timer went off and he opened the door to a small oven (about 4 ft. x 4 ft. x 6 ft.). He pulled a motorcycle frame out and hung it on a rack. A few minutes later he wrapped it in foam.

I was surprised. My experience painting cars was that after it's painted, it needs several days to dry. But this guy handled and wrapped this powder-coated finish in mere minutes. I was truly amazed. We concluded the meeting with him telling me it would be ten to twelve weeks before he could do anything for me.

THE BUILD

I left frustrated, but my wheels were turning. Two local companies with lead times of six to twelve weeks told me there was room for completion. Over the next couple of days, I contacted a supplier of powder coating equipment and ordered the PCI (Powder Coating Institute) Powder Coating Handbook. And Laurie and I started praying and fasting about starting this business.

I devoured the PCI handbook and researched all I could in two days. (Did I mention that I am impulsive and high energy?) Then I called the equipment supplier and asked if there was a consultant I could meet with. Preferably, someone who owns a powder coating shop where I could get my hands dirty. He told me of a couple of company owners who do consulting. I called one in Kansas City. His cost was $125/hour, and for that, he would tell me anything I wanted to know.

That night at dinner, I told Laurie all about what the consultant had told me. I told her I figured it would probably cost about $1,200 by the time I flew there and spent 4 hours at their shop. Laurie asked if we had the $1,200 in savings. I said we did. Then she said something profound.

"Isn't $1,200 a lot cheaper than spending hundreds of thousands of dollars on a company you know nothing about?"

She was absolutely correct. Two days later, I was on a plane to Kansas City. Laurence, the consultant, explained how he started with a small batch system and planned in six months to add a conveyorized powder system. That made great sense to me.

I returned home and Laurie and I continued to pray about starting the business. My theory is always to move forward until God says stop, so I started looking at buildings to rent and calling equipment manufacturers. It had been three weeks since I got the idea to start a powder coating shop. I realized that if I leased a building, at some point I'd eventually be moving all the heavy equipment again when I finally bought a building. So, I looked at a piece of property to purchase in our local industrial park. Within a few days, we bought it.

My plan was like Laurence's plan in Kansas City—start a batch system and in six months, add the conveyor system.

Bill, my partner in our exothermic powder business, agreed to run the dinosaur company we owned, and I would remain a stockholder and consult as needed. This freed me to pursue the powder coating company.

It had been six weeks from the time I visited those powder coating companies until we bought the land. I now turned my attention to getting a building erected and procuring the equipment. In June, we incorporated as A Plus Powder Coaters, Inc. I wanted a name that started with A so we would be the first shop in the yellow pages. (Back then there was no internet; people used phone books.)

In July, Laurie and I were getting ready to head to Thailand to adopt the first of two adopted children. Just three days before we were to leave, I went to a City Planning meeting to get permission to build a powder coating shop in the industrial park. They approved my plan and the newspaper ran a little story of A Plus Powder Coaters, Inc., a new startup in the Columbiana Industrial Park. The next day, I got a call from a local company needing powder coating and lots of it. As Laurie and I were on our way to Thailand, I told her more about what this company wanted. When I ran the numbers, I realized we could not do all the work in our batch system. We really needed the conveyor system we planned to install in six months after we started with the batch system. This is when Laurie said another profound statement.

"Is there really any difference if we borrow the money in six months or borrow it now?"

Wow! She was right again. I married a smart woman!

We returned from Thailand with our daughter and began looking for the equipment to build the conveyor system. In November of 1996, I had an office trailer moved next to the 11,250 square foot building we were having built. I hired Kathy, a friend from church, to be my office manager. Kathy, Laurie and I came up with our mission statement.

> *A Plus Powder Coaters, Inc. offers a high-quality product due to our commitment to Jesus Christ and our pledge to be good stewards of all God has blessed us with.*

FUTURE SO BRIGHT, GOTTA WEAR SHADES

Stewardship was something I cared about 20 years ago, and it has only grown since. We started A Plus with three employees, 11,250 square feet on two acres with no customers and no business strategy. As of this writing, we have grown to 40 employees, 60,000 square feet on 9.3 acres with hundreds of customers. It's been a wild ride.

At the end of 2012, we paid off all our loans. In 2014, we had tons of work, plenty of cash and were running out of room in our 40,000 square foot building.

Laurie and I started praying about expanding again. We decided to add a 20,000 square foot building, using half the area for our sandblast area and half for a warehouse. This would be our biggest single expansion ever. In November of 2014, we broke ground. The building was finished at the end of February 2015.

Our workload remained strong, so I bought two new forklifts, two 50hp air compressors with air driers, added a new 15 ft x 30 ft sandblast booth with a state-of-the-art dust collector, rebuilt our old sandblast room with another dust collector and added a new batch powder coating line.

Three and a third acres became available adjacent to our property, so we bought that too. I'm not bragging (well, maybe a little), but my point is that we were spending money back then—a lot of money. I was heavily involved in setting up and building our new equipment. It is what I love to do. Further, we were able to pay cash for the building and some of the equipment.

At this point, business began to slow. I was aware of it but not overly concerned. We'd seen ups and downs before. Besides, I was engaged with installing our new equipment. In early September, I finished the last system (the new powder batch system) and started to spend more time looking at our sales, market and expenses. That's when the shock set in. Things had slowed down way more than I realized. We actually had to borrow some money on our line of credit to finish the last few purchases. That's a common thing in business, but it was something I had hoped to avoid on this expansion. As October came around, things got even slower. I wasn't sure we would reach breakeven (the point where sales equal expenses).

I felt it in my gut. As a business owner with 40 people counting on me for a paycheck, heading into the holidays and then the traditionally slow first quarter (January – March), plus bills piling up, there was a little pressure.

Well, maybe a lot.

BY MY SPIRIT

Laurie and I had been invited to the HAPN (Heartland Apostolic Prayer Network) annual conference held in Oklahoma City at the end of October. We had committed to going months before things had started slowing down. I wasn't sure I wanted to go. My mind was really on how to help the business. *Do I lay off some workers? Shut down part of the factory? Rent out space?*

It was hard to focus on anything else, but since we were there at HAPN, I asked Nancy Foreit to pray for me. She has been known to pray for people's minds and they become healed. I knew I struggle with ADHD. It has always been difficult for me to sit still, stay focused and listen at conferences. Nancy prayed for me and I began to do better. Later that evening when the conference was over, she came up to me and we started talking.

She asked how my business was doing. I explained I might have to lay people off for the first time ever and it was weighing heavy on me, especially with Thanksgiving and Christmas coming up. What kind of jerk lays people off right before the Holidays?

Then she said, "You need to give it away."

I wasn't impressed.

What? Yeah, I know. Give it to the Lord. Lay it on the altar. Bleh, bleh, bleh.

If she could read me, she didn't let on as she continued in a warm, assuring tone.

"I owned my house but gave it to the Lord. It is his, not mine. When the refrigerator broke, I said, 'Father God, the house you own has a broken refrigerator; what are you going to do about it?' When my roof leaked, 'Father God, your house has a leaky roof; what are you going to do about it?'"

A light went on in my head! She was talking about stewardship, the responsible management of something entrusted to one's care. That was the answer I needed. I was so excited; I couldn't stop thinking about stewardship, what it meant and what it would look like from this point on.

I could hardly sleep that night. The next day at the conference, I couldn't get it out of my mind, so I ended up in the corner of the foyer with my iPad, typing out everything God was speaking to me about stewardship. Again, I had to repent for taking ownership and assuming the role of provider. Instead, I took my place as a steward.

"Father your business is losing money. It is not my business anymore. It is yours. What are you going to do about it?"

The weight lifted from my shoulders. It wasn't my responsibility to provide my employees with a paycheck or pay the company's bills. It was God's responsibility.

It felt wonderful and freeing to take my rightful place as a steward with a new perspective of stewardship. I started writing the Decree of Ownership that day. It took a week or so to get it to where I wanted it. I had it professionally printed. Then I signed it and hung it by the door to my office as a constant reminder of my position and responsibilities.

When I wrote the Decree of Ownership, I wasn't sure if it should be a declaration or a decree. A declaration is "a formal or explicit statement or announcement." Strong words. A decree is "an enforceable order based on legal authority." That resonated with me. Something that would be legal in the courts of heaven. I went with *decree*.

I had my pastor sign as my witness.

(Note: the Decree of Ownership is available on our website:

finishlineresources.com)

ALL'S WELL THAT ENDS WELL

I would love to tell you everything turned around that day, that sales went through the roof and life was great at A Plus Powder Coating, but that's not what happened.

Back in May of that year, before the October conference, I told God: "I am not as dependent on you as I use to be. I have no debt. We have good cash flow. I want to be dependent on you like I was when I started the company and depended on you to meet all our needs."

Sounds good, doesn't it? Well, all I can say is: *Be careful what you pray.* By the end of November (a month after the conference), instead of breaking even, we were losing tens of thousands of dollars.

In the midst of this story of tough times, allow me to brag about my team at A Plus. We had just done a cultural remodel 18 months prior. We had gotten rid of all the people with negative attitudes and established values that our employees came up with: <u>Respect, Attitude and Quality</u>. These are the things they wanted to be known for. We even came up with a new mission statement, "Be our best, for everyone's success!" (Catchy, eh?) The team believed if our customers were successful, the company would be successful. And if their co-workers were successful, everyone would be successful.

STRAIGHT UP

I called this great team together in mid-November and gave it to them straight. Sales were low, we were losing money and we may have to lay off some people. Then I pitched my best hope for the future: "Let's work as efficiently as possible and look for areas of inefficiency in our processes or practices that cost the company money."

I wanted to be up-front with my team, so I said: "If we lay anyone off, it will be by the least productive, not the least seniority."

Then I asked: "If anyone has any ideas about how we could save money or be more productive, please tell me."

Over the next 24 hours, three employees approached me with the idea of cutting everyone's hours to avoid laying anyone off. These guys were a team and were looking out for each other. I spent some time crunching numbers and realized that this would get us close to what we needed to save.

I called both shifts together and asked what they thought of cutting back to 36 hours a week? They all liked the idea much better than seeing anyone laid off. We all agreed to cut hours. I told them that as my part of the sacrifices we were all making, I wouldn't cut my hours, but I would not take a paycheck until they were all back to 40-hour weeks.

December was another bad month during which we lost tens of thousands of dollars, but I was ok with it. It wasn't my problem. It was God's.

"God, your company is losing money; what are you going to do about it? What is my role? Is there something I need to do? Is there something I need to repent for? Show me what you want me to do today."

It wasn't until the end of January that things picked back up. But during the time we were losing money, I was at peace. In fact, our neighbors, who we used to go out to dinner and play cards with almost every weekend for 40 years, commented, "I have seen you when your business has been down in the past, but this time, it hasn't affected you. You don't seem to be burdened as in times past. That stewardship change is really working."

Laurie made the same observation. Let's face it, men. When things are not going well, we can hold it together at work, but when we get home, we have little restraint. Previously in tough times, when I was at home, Laurie could barely ask "How are you?" before I'd snap back, "How do you think I am? My business is losing money!"

But this time was different. I was stress-free and carefree. It was God's problem. I rested in the fact that it was not my responsibility to fix it. Laurie, who has stood with me for over 33 years and really knows who I am, can attest to the change God brought through this experience. I am truly sorry I did not find this truth and depth of stewardship earlier in life. Laurie would not have had to live through some bad times with me being a grouch.

As of this writing, it has been a year since God renewed the principle of stewardship in my life. At God's company, A Plus Powder Coaters, Inc., sales have been up and down. Most of our customers are down 20% to 50% in sales. We are down 8.3% for the year. Some months we make some money and some months we lose money. I am ok with that. I am still at a place of peace and rest, knowing it is God's responsibility. It is his company.

GOD'S CARE FOR US

Earlier in this book, I told you that God is the provider. Allow me to tell you how God provided for Laurie and me when we had no salary for six months.

Laurie and I are empty nesters. Our kids have flown the coop and are on their own. We missed them terribly in the beginning but gradually became spoiled. We ate out most nights. We had no personal debt, just our utility bills and groceries. Life was good.

When business slowed and I decided not to take a paycheck, we decided we would trim our spending, not eat out so much, and watch our other expenses. Well, apparently God didn't think that was necessary, as he started supplying meals out at no cost. Let me explain.

My workers, whose hours we had cut back to 36 per week to keep from laying off, gave us $450 worth of restaurant gift cards for Christmas. That was so unexpected. I knew they all were making sacrifices with the cuts to their paychecks. I cried when I opened the envelope. I also found gift cards for restaurants in my coat pocket that I had forgotten I had. I found gift cards in my glove box and bathroom mirror that I forgot I had. We started just going to dinner where we had gift cards. On top of this, many times we would go out with other couples and they bought our dinner. They had no idea I had no income. Only my employees and a few close friends knew. I wasn't complaining to anyone about our situation. I believed God was my provider. I knew he would provide for me, income or no income.

One day, I was at the Chiropractor's office to have my back adjusted. When I went to pay, the receptionist said, "No charge." This happened several times. At another visit, the receptionist said someone had already paid for my visit. The Chiropractor had no idea I had no income; neither did the person who paid for one of my visits. God knew, and he provided.

I feel called as a financier of the Kingdom, giving to ministries. I had made many pledges to support these ministries over the years. When I had no income, I had the perfect excuse to quit giving to them, but I didn't. My wife and I have a separate account we call the *slush fund*. This is money set aside explicitly to give away. We never spend it on ourselves. God provided enough in our slush fund and savings to never miss a giving opportunity or commitment.

God is so faithful!

This experience grounded me even more in the truth that God is the provider and I am the steward.

11

Tithe

TITHE: *A tenth part of something paid as a voluntary contribution.*

A tithe is 10% of your gross wages. It's the minimum wage of giving, the only defined amount of any type of giving.

WHAT!!?

You heard me: <u>*I call tithe the minimum wage of giving.*</u>

Some of you are gasping for air. I get it. Please hear me out before you disregard what I am saying. I know without a doubt that these five keys work. They are the reason I'm here. My desire is to see the entire body of Christ enjoy what God intends for us.

It's simple, really. God wants 10% of his money back. It's part of our commitment to God. He must be first in our lives. That includes our finances. Remember, it is his money anyway, so it shouldn't be a big deal to give back 10% of what doesn't belong to us in the first place.

Picture it like this. If I offered you $100, but all I asked in return was for you to give me back $10, would you accept my $100? You'd take the $100 and gladly give the $10 back. You came out with $90 you didn't have before. Pretty sweet deal, right?

I find it helpful when I write my tithe check (10% of my gross) to thank God for providing me with the other 90%. Also, since it is his money anyway, I want to be a good steward and spend it the way he desires.

God desires a tithe.

DISTRIBUTION

What is a tithe used for? Who gets it? Tithe goes to the place you are being spiritually fed—typically the church you attend. The entire tithe should go to one church, not divided up. It is up to the church to use as it sees fit, but generally, it pays pastors and overhead—the expenses of running a church.

Let's also clear up some misconceptions.

1. We do not use the tithe to manipulate the pastor or church. It is not given as an approval of what the pastor or church is doing or saying.

"I disagree with what Pastor John said last week, so I am not tithing."

"Pastor, if you will do this, I will give a tithe to the church."

These are all forms of manipulation—a form of witchcraft, according to the Bible. We tithe to honor God and be obedient to his word. I have told people at our church: "If you're giving to manipulate, it's tainted money and we don't want it."

2. If you give a tithe and designate it for a specific fund, it isn't really a tithe; it is an offering. You see, the tithe is for the church to decide how to use it. You have no say it over it. (We'll cover offerings later.)

TITHE IN SCRIPTURE

Let's look at some scriptures about tithing.

> A tithe of everything from the land, whether grain from the soil or fruit from the trees, belongs to the Lord; it is holy to the Lord.
>
> Leviticus 27:30 NIV

Be sure to set aside a tenth of all that your fields produce each year.

Deuteronomy 14:22 NIV

These scriptures tell us we need to tithe. Please keep in mind that when these scriptures were written, grain, fruit and livestock were all considered currency.

Now consider the scripture that is most often used when speakers want to scare us into giving. "I the Lord do not change" (Malachi 3:6 NIV).

The first thing God tells us is that he is consistent. Why is that important? Because he wants us to know that what he said in the past is still relevant today. We are to assume that what he is about to tell us is still true. Let's follow his word:

"I the Lord do not change. So you, the descendants of Jacob, are not destroyed. Ever since the time of your ancestors you have turned away from my decrees and have not kept them. Return to me, and I will return to you," says the Lord Almighty.

"But you ask, 'How are we to return?'

"Will a mere mortal rob God? Yet you rob me.

"But you ask, 'How are we robbing you?'

"In tithes and offerings. You are under a curse—your whole nation—because you are robbing me. Bring the whole tithe into the storehouse, that there may be food in my house."

Malachi 3:6-10 NIV

God gives his people a chance to return to him. That is one of the things I love about God. He gives us second chances (and third, fourth, fifth...). He doesn't condemn us just because we screw up. He desires us to return to him. In Malachi, he was asking the people to obey what was required of them—in this case, to bring the tithe to the storehouse.

> *"Test me in this," says the Lord Almighty, "and see if I will not throw open the floodgates of heaven and pour out so much blessing that there will not be room enough to store it. I will prevent pests from devouring your crops, and the vines in your fields will not drop their fruit before it is ripe," says the Lord Almighty. "Then all the nations will call you blessed, for yours will be a delightful land," says the Lord Almighty.*

Malachi 3:10-12 NIV

Here is where I get excited. God says *test me in this*. I never recommend testing God on something. (Wasn't there a temptation of Jesus like that?) He is God and will win. But here, he gives us permission to test him. He is all but begging for his people to trust him and return to him.

Now earlier, I talked about the transfer of wealth. Here is another scripture pointing to that. "See if I will not throw open the floodgates of heaven and pour out so much blessing that there will not be room to store it."

That's a lot of blessing. So, what is the key to receiving all that blessing?

Tithing.

In verse 11, we read: "I will prevent pests from devouring your crops."

God says he will prevent pests from devouring our crops. *That's nice, but I'm not a farmer, so I have no crops.* But what do *crops* represent? In Old Testament times, bartering was used to trade and acquire things. A farmer might trade grain for a goat, or two goats for a bull. It was a form of currency. So, in this scripture, God is saying he will prevent our money from being devoured.

Do you ever feel like your paycheck is devoured? Gone and spent as soon as you get it? Perhaps you need to tithe.

TITHE IN PRACTICE

I recently found a distressing statistic. Only 5-7% of Christians tithe. I couldn't believe it. Only 5-7% of Christians tithe? You're probably thinking that includes all denominations—protestant, catholic, orthodox, and everything in between. Surely, born-again, Bible-believing, miracle-seeking Christians tithe at a higher rate. You're absolutely correct! A whopping 9% of born-again Christians tithe.

It broke my heart. How can this be? Then I found it. A mere 5% of pastors tithe.

No wonder the church doesn't tithe. It really started to make me mad that pastors are denying the church the opportunity to be blessed and shown favor by God for tithing. But it is no wonder. The pastors don't even tithe. What a shame! They are taking that opportunity away from us because they don't understand the simple truth of God's stewardship.

I hope to change that.

I was at a conference and spoke briefly about tithing. A pastor came up to me and asked, "Should a church tithe?" I said I felt they should, and I told how God had increased our congregation size and income at our church after they started tithing. She said they used to tithe, but their congregation had shrunk and they didn't think they could afford it so they stopped tithing.

Later at the conference, this pastor came up to me ecstatic. She told me their church used to tithe to the church that was holding the conference. They felt the need to start tithing again. So, they went to the pastor of the church and repented for stopping the tithe and handed the pastor a tithe check. While she was handing the check, someone tapped the tithing pastor on the shoulder and said, "I want to sow into your ministry." The next day someone else approached them and handed them another check. These were the first major contributions the church had seen in years.

Is God faithful or what?

MY STORY OF TITHING

I started tithing when I got saved at age 14. It was easy for me. I lived at home and had no bills. I needed money for fun stuff: restaurants, guitars and skiing, but giving 10% was no big deal. I had a hard time understanding why someone wouldn't tithe.

My perspective has recently changed, however, and I want to share my experience with you. Now I get why people struggle.

I was at the HAPN (Heartland Apostolic Prayer Network) annual conference in October 2017, listening to Faisal Malick speak on finances. He mentioned something that pricked my heart. It was about the distinction between personal tithing and business tithing.

As a business owner, I am technically the steward of a business owned by God. Any income I have ever taken from the company, I tithed on, no questions asked. But Faisal's mention of company tithing intrigued me. You see, up until this point, I viewed companies as an extension of my life. But what Faisal said really got me thinking.

When I got home from the conference, I started asking God if he wanted A Plus Powder Coaters to tithe, and if so, what number? Gross sales? Net profit? Projected earnings?

I confess that when I thought of tithing from gross sales, that scared me a little...ok, maybe a lot. Ten percent of gross sales would be close to our yearly profit, even greater for some years.

I prayed and meditated on it for many days. *God, what do you require of me? What do you require of the business?* I wanted to do what God wanted, even if I didn't think it was possible. *God, give me the faith to tithe as you want me to.*

I finally called Faisal for a more in-depth discussion. I asked him why he thought a business should tithe, and scripturally, what he based this on? He told me Abraham tithed off of what his servants brought in from the harvest. His servants were like our modern-day employees. They work for us just like Abraham's servants harvested for him. Our harvest is profits. That made sense.

I then asked what we should tithe from? Gross sales? Profits? He said this depended on the business. He has some companies that are all service or labor. In those cases, he tithes off the gross sales. He also has other businesses that sell his books. For these, he subtracts the cost of goods from before he tithes. If he sells a book for $10 and it cost him $4, he tithes off the $6 he made. I understood his reasoning, so I was pretty sure I would tithe off the business, but I still didn't have a peace on what parameter to tithe from.

It was now December and I was still asking God to reveal his heart to me. I was having breakfast one morning with Perry, one of our church pastors. Perry is a banker who works on the commercial lending side of banking. I told him I felt God was calling me to tithe from A Plus, but I wasn't sure from what basis. Gross sales? Profits? He said he thought maybe profits.

As I continued to pray and think about this, I called John Benefiel from HAPN, as I knew he had been in the business world before starting a church and HAPN. John offered some insights and thought tithing from A Plus was a good thing to do. He said his initial thought was to tithe from profits.

It is now just before Christmas and I still didn't have a clear-cut answer. I call my accountant and asked if he could put a small spreadsheet together with the last few years of gross sales vs. profit. On the Tuesday before Christmas, he sent the file over. As I looked at it, the profit number for the previous year did not match what we had talked about the week before. So, I called him, and he explained that the spreadsheet was showing net income. This was all the profit before we deducted anything on my taxes or the rapid depreciation of equipment. This meant that if I spent $50,000 on equipment, I could deduct it from the net income and not pay taxes. It also did not include any deductions for charitable contributions. This number resonated with me.

Tuesday evening at dinner, I told Laurie what I felt we should do. She was onboard. Wednesday morning in my prayer time, I repented to God for not tithing from A Plus before this. I said that starting January 1, I would tithe on the company net income.

That's when God took it up a gear. Have you ever had God drop a thought in your mind, something profound? That's what happened that morning.

I felt God say: "If you had just cheated on your wife, went to her and repented, then told her that in a week and a half you would make things right, how would that work out?"

Not so well. If I really repented, the change would happen immediately, not at a future date. So, I went to my office and wrote a tithe check for the previous year. I did not know this current year's net income until April when the taxes were done.

That evening, Laurie and I were scheduled to go to a staff Christmas party at Perry and Joy's house. I was invited because Laurie is on the pastoral staff. I asked Laurie if we could go early, as I needed to repent to Perry and Joy. We arrived a few minutes before anyone else showed up. I asked them to forgive me for robbing the storehouse by not tithing from A Plus. They released me and said it isn't a sin until we commit it after we know it's wrong. I said I still needed to make it right in the Father's eyes by coming to them. That's when I handed them my tithe check for the previous year.

Here's what happened after I gave that tithe check.

December was a fair month in sales. December 15th through about January 15th are generally slower since many fabrication shops close up and don't produce anything for us to coat during the holidays. January started off slow at A Plus, as usual. But on the 15th, the floodgates opened. We set a new company sales record for a month. Sales went up just over 70% from December and 56% from the previous year's monthly average. That's huge! In the 30+ years I've been in business, I've never seen that much growth in one month. I have seen maybe 20% - 25% increase, but never over 70%. In February, we set another sales record, up over 20% from January and over 90% from the previous year's average.

I am amazed at God and his faithfulness. I sure wish I would have tithed from A Plus from the first day we started.

If you haven't been tithing, I believe it is time to first repent for being disobedient, and second, to start tithing. When you get paid, write a check for ten percent of your gross wage to the church you go to. I know this can be a little scary, especially if you have been living paycheck to paycheck. It may not make sense, but I know God is faithful and his word is true.

It's time to tithe.

12

Give

I WAS CREATED TO GIVE to ministries. This is one of my callings—to be a financer of the Kingdom. In following this calling, I have studied giving and witnessed the effect of giving on people's lives—both givers and receivers.

There are many truths specific to giving. When we honor God by giving back to him, he sees us as good stewards and provides more for us to steward. As you read earlier, Laurie and I are givers. I credit much of our financial success to that fact. We strive to be good stewards.

I want to share some of the things I have learned about giving and the different types of giving. It starts with remembering that it's God's money, not ours. We need to be good stewards with the financial resources with which God entrusts us.

Now, some of my readers may want to stop at this point and toss this book. So many of us tune out when it comes to giving. Have you ever heard (or said), "I can't afford to tithe or give"? My answer, borne of a lifetime of experience, is that you can't afford *not to* tithe and give.

Please hang with me for a short time and try to have an open mind. If, at the end, you want to go back to your way of thinking, you can. In the meantime, let's consider the different types of giving, their purposes and rewards.

ALMS

Alms, definition: "Something (such as money or food) given freely to relieve the poor. Charity."

This refers to giving that is separate from your tithe, above and beyond. Your tithe cannot be designated as alms. It is what Matthew refers to: "So when you give to the needy" (Matthew 6:2 NIV). The key is giving to the needy—the homeless, a homeless shelter, soup kitchen, food pantry, clothing ministry, anyone in need within the church or beyond.

> But if there are any poor Israelites in your towns when you arrive in the land the Lord your God is giving you, do not be hard-hearted or tightfisted toward them. Instead, be generous and lend them whatever they need. Do not be mean-spirited and refuse someone a loan because the year for canceling debts is close at hand. If you refuse to make the loan and the needy person cries out to the Lord, you will be considered guilty of sin. Give generously to the poor, not grudgingly, for the Lord your God will bless you in everything you do. There will always be some in the land who are poor. That is why I am commanding you to share freely with the poor and with other Israelites in need.
>
> Deuteronomy 15:7-11 NLT

We are told three things in this passage.

1. Give generously to the poor.
2. Give with a good attitude, not grudgingly.
3. God will bless you in everything you do.

The NIV says:

> *Give generously to them and do so without a grudging heart; then because of this the Lord your God will bless you in all your work and in everything you put your hand to.*

Deuteronomy 15:10 NIV

God will bring good to us in all our work and everything we do. That is amazing! Can God's goodness get much easier? Give to the poor and he will bless our work and everything we do. That's easy money.

OFFERINGS

Offerings, definition: "A thing offered, especially as a gift or contribution."

Offerings are funds given to specific things such as a building fund, missionaries, outreach projects, disaster relief or collections for someone who lost their home. They can also be special giving to help the church out in some unique way.

We read in the Gospel of Mark:

> *Jesus sat down opposite the place where the offerings were put and watched the crowd putting their money into the temple treasury. Many rich people threw in large amounts.*

Mark 12:41 NIV

FIRST FRUITS

First Fruits, definition: "The earliest fruit of the season."

Alms and offerings are fairly common in the church setting. First fruits, however, don't seem to be talked about as much, but I believe they are still for today's Christians and an important key to our whole financial blessing.

From the New Testament:

> *As soon as the order went out, the Israelites generously gave the first fruits of their grain, new wine, olive oil and honey and all that the fields produced. They brought a great amount, a tithe of everything.*

2 Chronicles 31:5 NIV

Many people believe first fruits and tithe are one in the same. I have even heard people refer to their tithe as first fruits. This is not correct, however. The first-fruit offering was given at the beginning of the harvest, hence *first fruits*. When they brought in the first of the crops, they took some and gave a first-fruits offering. We need to remember that back then, they did not have large farm equipment to bring in the harvest, only large oxen. It took weeks to get it all done, and they faced challenges: weather, pestilence, even enemies raiding the fields. So, they gave a first-fruits offering at the beginning of the harvest as a means of sowing into God to reap a bountiful harvest.

The first-fruits offering could not be the tithe, since they would not have known the total of their harvest until after it was all harvested. So, they tithed at the end of the harvest, but they gave a first-fruits offering at the beginning of the harvest.

What might first fruits look like to us today? For Laurie and I, we give a first-fruit offering in the fall. We look at the Jewish calendar and give according to when the Jews would have given theirs. We give one for ourselves and one for our company, A Plus.

We also give one at the beginning of the calendar year. We are sowing into God providing for us. And boy has he!

At a financial conference, I spoke one morning on giving and sowing a first-fruits offering from your business. At the end of the day, a very excited lady came up to me. She said that while I was speaking, she felt her business needed to give a first-fruits offering. She texted her office manager and instructed her to give an offering to a church. During the afternoon session of the conference, she got a call. They just got two new clients and might have to hire another employee. God is good. This business owner sowed in the morning and reaped the benefits that afternoon. Thank you, Jesus!

WHY OR HOW WE GIVE

Had you asked me this question five years ago, I would have told you there is only one reason to give. But over the last couple of years, God has revealed several reasons for giving. I am going to start with the one I have believed for a long time.

A. Obedience

God wants us to be obedient. Just as a father wants his children to obey, God wants us to obey Him.

Parents, here's a question: Would you allow your teenager to operate a 4,000-pound killing machine?

If you're like me, you would. It's called a car, and it's capable of killing your teenager, their friends, people in other cars and any bystanders. In fact, it happens every day by the hundreds. But we still trust our children with these machines.

Would you agree that part of a teenager earning that privilege is that they consistently demonstrate obedient and responsible behavior? Or course you would. Father God is the same way. He wants to know we will obey him and his word.

> _Whoever can be trusted with very little can also be trusted with much, and whoever is dishonest with very little will also be dishonest with much._

Luke 16:10 NIV

If we are obedient in little, we will be obedient with much.

Earlier in this chapter, we read scriptures telling us to tithe, give alms, offerings and first-fruits offerings. Are we obedient to these things? God even said to test him in tithes. Have we been obedient in testing him? It only works when you obey.

B. Act of Love

Recently, I have discovered a new reason for giving—an act of love. Giving is an expression of our love for God.

Here's how I relate to it. I love my wife. I try to tell her several times a day so she can't forget it. But it gets monotonous to repeat, "I love you, Laurie, I love you, Laurie, I love you, Laurie" all day. How else can I express my love?

Well, we spend money on the things we love, right? I know I do. I spend money on my wife. I buy her flowers and cards. I take her dinner. We go on vacation. I even buy her Tootsie Pops. Yeah, I know—big spender. But it blesses her and tells her I love her.

We spend money on what we love. Yet do we spend money on God? Do we give to his work? Show me your bank statement and I'll show you your heart. Where does our money go? To the things we value: mortgage, car payment, groceries. Who doesn't like to live in a house, drive a decent car and eat rather than starve! But wait, there's more: hobbies, toys, trips. All work and no play make Jack a dull boy, right? And there's giving to our church, missions, the homeless and building funds.

All these are things we love. Follow the money and you'll discover the heart.

It's time we show God our love by giving.

C. Act of Worship

Giving is an act of worship. It shows God that we think he is more important than wealth. He *should be* way more important than wealth. This is similar to an act of love. We all worship something. Many of us worship money. We spend our lives and energy going after it. It is our heart's desire. We can't get enough of it. It's our safety net. It might even become our god (mammon) if we let it.

We need to worship God with our giving. This demonstrates to God that he is more important than even wealth. Have you ever been in God's presence and you say, "God, you are my all-in-all. You are my everything!" A true test of that statement is this: Do you worship him with your wealth?

D. Covenant

Covenant, definition: "A usually formal, solemn, and binding agreement."

Our giving is a covenant with God.

In the Bible, a covenant is a solemn, binding agreement between God and us. I once heard Faisal Malick say, "Tithe is the wedding ring of our covenant with Jesus. It binds us to Jesus."

How cool is that? I am in covenant with Jesus, all because of my tithe and offerings.

BENEFITS OF GIVING

This is my favorite part. I have a lot to say about this and I get excited. So, let's get right to it.

A. ROI (Return On Investment)

Now, you know I am a businessman. As such, I am always looking for what my ROI is. If I spend $10,000 on a new machine, what will my return be? Will it make money or consume money? If it makes $5,000 a year, I will break even in two years and make money the third year. But if it only makes $500 a year, I'm not likely to ever make money before it breaks down and gets sold for scrap metal.

Well, we also get an ROI on our giving. Look at Proverbs:

Honor the Lord with your wealth, with the firstfruits of all your crops; then your barns will be filled to overflowing, and your vats will brim over with new wine.

Proverbs 3:9-10 NIV

Here we are told if we honor the Lord with our wealth and give a first-fruits offering, we will have barns filled to overflowing and vats filled to the brim with new wine. In other words, when I give a first-fruits offering, God is going to pour back into me more finances.

Did you also notice that it said, "Honor the Lord with your wealth?" We honor God with our wealth when he is first and our money and finances are a distant second. If our goal is just about getting wealth and having more, then we are making it mammon, the god of money, and we are not honoring God. It's with a pure heart for God, putting him first in our lives, that we honor Him.

*Test me in this," says the Lord Almighty, "and see
if I will not throw open the floodgates of heaven
and pour out so much blessing that there will not
be room enough to store it.*

Malachi 3:10 NIV

If we tithe, our ROI is seeing God "throw open the floodgates of heaven and pour out so much blessing that there will not be room enough to store it." God seems to give back very generously.

For many, this scripture in Luke is the gold standard for giving:

*Give, and it will be given to you. A good measure,
pressed down, shaken together and running over,
will be poured into your lap. For with the measure
you use, it will be measured to you.*

Luke 6:38 NIV

If we give, it will be given back to us. How exciting is that?! We give out of love, worship and obedience, and God returns even more. It doesn't get much simpler.

The truth of these promises is borne out empirically. Here are some statistics backing up God's words to us.

Of the people who tithe:

- 80% have no unpaid credit card bills
- 74% owe nothing on their cars
- 48% own their homes
- 28% are debt-free

Wow, that is impressive. I credit Laurie's and my giving with enabling us to fit into all these categories. God is so good! If you don't fit into any of these categories yet, perhaps it's time to start tithing and giving. Then watch what happens.

B. Builds Memorials

> *Cornelius stared at him in fear. "What is it, Lord?" he asked. The angel answered, "Your prayers and gifts to the poor have come up as a memorial offering before God."*

> Acts 10:4 NIV

Before we go on, we need to understand what we mean by *memorial*.

Memorial, definition: "Something designed to preserve the memory of a person, event, etc."

When we pray and give gifts, we build memorials before the Lord. I would like to have memorials before the Lord—things he remembers me for. If our prayers aren't being answered, maybe we need to give and pray so memorials will be built before the Lord.

Notice what God rewarded here—prayers and gifts to the poor. Because Cornelius was a gentile, he could not go into a Jewish temple. Therefore, Cornelius could not tithe to a local church, as there were no gentile churches that followed Christ at the time. There were only Jewish temples. Still, Cornelius believed in God and gave to the poor, and a memorial was built before God.

C. Spiritual Warfare

Giving prevents spiritual warfare. Faisal Malick: "Spiritual warfare is diminished when we tithe. When we don't tithe, we open ourselves up to spiritual warfare." I don't know about you, but if I can avoid spiritual warfare, I'm all about that. I want the least amount possible, so if giving prevents it, I'm giving.

D. Financial Protection

When we give, it protects our finances.

> *I will prevent pests from devouring your crops, and the vines in your fields will not drop their fruit before it is ripe," says the Lord Almighty.*

> Malachi 3:11 NIV

The Lord prevents pests from devouring our financial resources. Not only does God give us an ROI on our giving, but he protects what he has already given us. If we don't give, it gives legal right for the enemy to devour our resources.

WHY DON'T PEOPLE TITHE?

I've always wondered why people don't tithe. Is it too scary? Is it because it doesn't make sense? What is it? Finally, from my experience wrestling with whether or not to tithe from our business, A Plus, I came to appreciate what others may wrestle with.

In January, I decided to fast for three days. One of the things I was fasting for was to understand what prevents people from tithing. As I journaled the first morning, I asked God why people don't tithe.

Now, I had just walked through the process of tithing on my business, so the subject was fresh on my mind. On the third day of the fast, as I journaled, the word *trust* came to mind. As I pondered trust, I realized we don't trust who we don't know. Allow me to elaborate on this.

Let's start with knowing God vs knowing *of* God. Here's how it works.

I know my wife, Laurie. She likes flowers; Gerbera daisies are her favorite. She loves her quiet time every morning. She likes Tootsie Pops and grape is her favorite flavor. She likes to go out to dinner whenever possible. She likes small intimate groups of people, not large parties. I know these things about her because I know *her*. We've lived a lifetime together and I know the person, Laurie.

On the other hand, I know *of* Jay Leno. I have seen him on the *Tonight Show* and on *Jay Leno's Garage*. I know we are both car guys and that his collection is bigger than mine. But if I were to pass by Jay somewhere, I would not go up to him and ask if he wants to go to his favorite restaurant, because I don't know his favorite restaurant. I don't know much about him because we don't know each other. I know of him, but I don't know him.

Many Christians are the same way. They know *of* God, they even know (and love) *the things of* God. But, if they are not givers, could it be that they really don't know Father God?

They may consider themselves true worshippers of God. They may have been in ministry for decades or studied the Bible their whole lives. They may even experience God in intimate worship or be able to recite every key verse in the Bible, but in the area of finances, do they know God?

If we really knew God, we would know his word is true. Although we are called to tithe and give, we are also told that God gives back. If we knew God, we would know that just as an earthly father loves to see his children obey, so does our Heavenly Father. Just as I enjoy giving my daughters gifts and blessing them, so our Heavenly Father enjoys giving us gifts and blessing us.

The key, then, is to pursue God himself, not just for what he can do for us, but for who he is. We can't trust a stranger, even a benevolent stranger, but we can trust those we know—those with whom we spend our lives and invest our hearts. The gifts, then, become the side effects. The quest is the heart of God.

TRUST IN GOD OR MONEY

As I pondered trusting God, I realized many people trust money more than God. I know I mentioned this earlier, but it needs to be reiterated. If our security is in our bank account or knowing we can pay the bills with this week's check, we are trusting money to sustain our lifestyle. Our trust isn't in God as our provider. It should be.

> How could you worship two gods at the same time? You will have to hate one and love the other, or be devoted to one and despise the other. You can't worship the true God while enslaved to the god of money!

Matthew 6:24 TPT

Are we enslaved to the god of money? We can't worship both our Heavenly Father and mammon, the god of money. How much do we trust God with his money?

> Command those who are rich in this present world not to be arrogant nor to put their hope in wealth, which is so uncertain, but to put their hope in God, who richly provides us with everything for our enjoyment.

1 Timothy 6:17 NIV

Here again, our hope and trust must be in God, not money.

A man named Fredrick heard me speak on tithing from my business. He embraced the idea immediately and wrote out a tithe check from his business that very day. The next day, his phone erupted with calls and inquires. He saw me the next week and said he has never had so many calls in one week. He is now overwhelmed with work—a good problem to have.

Honoring God with our tithe works.

Remember: We are stewards; God owns everything, including our wealth. So...do we trust God with his money? If you struggle with the thought of tithing, I encourage you to be brave enough to ask God what he requires of you. Ask him to help you come to a place of knowing Him and trusting Him with everything, including your wealth.

13

Spend

To CREATE WEALTH, YOU HAVE TO SPEND. That's right...spend. If we have the right perspective of stewardship, God's ownership, tithing and giving, then we get to spend the rest.

But I won't have enough for my bills!

I beg to disagree.

You see, if we adhere to the understandings and practices mentioned previously, God will supply all our needs and we can spend it on all our needs.

Now, please don't think I am advocating that we buy anything and everything we want. I am saying there will be enough to meet and exceed our needs.

Our True Condition

Here are the facts on the financial state of most people.

- 78% percent of full-time workers said they live paycheck to paycheck. (CNBC Online)
- 71% of all U.S. workers said they're now in debt. (CNBC Online)
- 46% said their debt is manageable. (CNBC Online)
- 56% said they were in over their heads. (CNBC Online)
- 10% of those making $100,000 or more say they can't make ends meet. (CNBC Online)
- 46% of Americans cannot afford a $400 emergency. (Washington Post)

By these facts, it's clear that most people can't manage their money, including Christians. Surprisingly, 78% of full-time workers live paycheck to paycheck. Assuming wages gradually increase over time (raises, job changes, promotions, cost of living adjustments), it appears that as they earned more, they spent more. This is quite common.

When I was still learning how to give and spend, my wages went up 50% in one year. The following year, they doubled, and they doubled again the next year. Not surprisingly, when my wages went up, so did my spending. That's why I had no more in the bank than I had before the raises. I'm sure I'm not the exception.

As we struggle to learn to live within our means, we might need tools to help us. Budgets can be helpful when used properly. Now, I know that I am not as strong a proponent of budgets as other Christian teachers. My issue, however, is that for many years this was the only way the church preached stewardship. When I teach stewardship, I stress an attitude of controlling our lifestyles rather than micromanaging every cent. Still, budgets can be helpful, especially if we have not managed our finances well in the past.

If you are living paycheck to paycheck, I would venture to say you might need a budget. As a way to learn about budgets, I highly recommend Dave Ramsey's *Financial Peace Class*. Just be careful not to become too legalistic about it. There will be times that God will ask you to give more, and we can't respond by saying "It isn't in our budget." Remember, it's all God's money, not ours.

Learn to live within your means. Question every purchase, starting with: Do I have the cash to buy it? If you make $30,000 a year, you should not buy a $70,000 Cadillac or a $300,000 house.

Learn to be satisfied with a Kia and a simple house in a good neighborhood. Buy what you can afford, things that will meet your needs and provide good value in the long run, and trust God for the increase.

I WANT IT NOW!

The more I talk to people about finances the more I realize that many people are impulsive buyers. We see something and we must have it...NOW! Why wait until we can afford it? The bank will finance it for us! Perfect!! Until you assess the costs of borrowing.

We need to set some rules here. Only borrow money for assets—things that will appreciate in value. The opposite of an asset is a liability—something that depreciates with time.

Cars are generally liabilities. If you buy a new car, it depreciates 10% the moment you drive it off the lot and 20% in the first year. Even if it had only 10 miles on it, you would only get less than you paid because it is considered *used*. By the time five years of payments are done, the car is worth about half of what you paid for it. It is a liability, not an asset.

Pay cash for liabilities. For a car, buy what you can afford and begin saving for the next purchase. I know people who buy an older car with cash, then make a payment to their savings account each month rather than a car payment. This allows them to save for a newer car.

Of course, there are assets worth borrowing for. A house is the most common. Buy what you can afford and pay it off in the shortest time possible. There are various strategies for doing this. One is to pay extra on the principle. This lowers the loan amount, which in turn lowers the interest charged. It also increases the gain you can make when you sell the house, assuming it has increased in value.

Keep in mind, however, that there is no guarantee that you will make money on a house. A house can depreciate depending on several factors: the housing market, the credit market, the condition of the house or shifts in neighborhood desirability. The value of the urban townhouse you bought for $250,000 can go south quickly when a new interstate is routed 100 feet from the front door. So, buy carefully.

Businesses can be another asset worth borrowing money for. In our business, we have borrowed hundreds of thousands of dollars over the years, especially when we first started, and later when we expanded. Because we borrowed wisely, the additional equipment and buildings generated much more money than we borrowed. Yes, it was a risk. Borrowing money is always risky. That is why we are careful with our borrowing. It has to make sense from a business perspective. The reasonable assurance of an increased ROI has to be proven. Furthermore, I make it a practice to pay off all loans as soon as possible. I will even lower my salary to pay off more of the debt quickly.

I said I don't like to borrow for liabilities because they depreciate. Some things that fall into that category are appliances, TVs, furniture and lawnmowers. It is so tempting when merchants offer 0% financing for six months. Sounds like a wise move to use their money for free, but most people forget to set the money aside to pay off the loan, and the interest rate— typically higher than market—kicks in automatically. Remember, there is no such thing as *free* money. If there is no interest to the loan, you are either paying for it in a higher purchase price, or the seller is betting that you will not pay it in six months when the usurious rates kick in and you are caught without the means to pay off the loan.

People conveniently forget one obligation and spend the money on something else they *must have now*. Making matters worse, once they pass the six-month deadline, the interest accruals go back to the beginning of the loan. That great deal they got on their big screen TV ends up costing a lot more than they bargained for.

Let's face it—we are great at justifying why we need something immediately and how it will save us money. The first time our car needs to be repaired, we take out a new car loan with no money down and justify it with the "savings" of future auto repairs. In reality, we have eliminated one problem but gained a new problem—a monthly payment for the next 72 months that we really can't afford.

When Laurie and I were young, we shopped for new cars and quickly realized we couldn't afford them. Undeterred, the salesman tried to convince us that if we quit spending on a few things, we could afford the car payment. He rattled off a list of expendable items like a financial seminar speaker:

- Do you smoke? Quitting smoking would free up hundreds a month and you could afford a higher payment.
- Do you eat out? Going out to dinner one less time a month would free up $60 for your payment.
- Do you pack your lunch for work? That would free up $75 a month for your payment.
- Do you have children? Giving one of them away would...

Most of his advice was true (except the children, of course), but I wonder how many people actually stick to that plan once the loan takes over. How many people actually quit smoking to make their car payment? My guess is few to none. If the threat of death by cancer hasn't induced them to quit by now, would a car payment do it? Not hardly. The salesman's advice was just a ruse to make a sale.

How To Buy

Here's how to make purchases: Ask God to supply your needs. Ask him if now is the right time to buy that TV, the washer and dryer, the car, the house, the business, the exotic pet. As I mentioned earlier, I changed my prayers when I realized it was God's responsibility to provide. Your prayers might sound something like this:

- Lord, the car you own needs to be repaired. What are you going to do about it?
- Lord, your house has a broken furnace. What's your plan?
- Lord, your house has a water leak in the basement. When does the plumber arrive?

It respectfully puts the burdens where they belong: on the owner of the items—God. It is his job to provide. If we will ask God and listen, he will speak and/or provide for the situation...as long as we are following all the precepts we discussed here.

What about when we want something new, like a new car? I would ask God if that is what he wants for us, and then ask him to provide it. Try not to be impatient with God. Don't just pray in the morning and run out and buy one when the dealership opens, unless that is what God said to do. Learn to listen for God to speak and discover how he wants to provide. Don't be impatient and impulsive. God will provide what you need and desire.

Modern, affluent culture is an entitled culture. The mantra is: *I deserve it. Therefore, I should have it NOW!* As Christians, we must guard our hearts and minds against falling into the entitlement mindset. We are not owed anything. It is all a gift and blessing from God.

Live within your means. You know what you make and what you will have after you have tithed, given alms and offerings. Expect God to bless you but remember that part of that blessing is in preventing loss.

God promises to rebuke the devourer, and his word is true. Although you may not see God's protection as an increase in your bank account, you will see it in other ways. Your cars will last longer, your houses will need fewer repairs, and your lifestyle will be less costly. Overall, God's protection will keep you from the financial struggles that others face: unemployment, legal issues, divorce. I'm not saying Christians, or even tithers and givers, never see difficult things. I'm saying that comparatively speaking, God's protection extends far beyond what we may notice in the immediate.

Let us be wise in our spending, temperate in our expectations and give God the glory in all things.

14

Thankfulness

PEOPLE WHO KNOW ME say I am thankful and appreciative for nearly everything. Most of my prayers start with "Thank you, Lord." I do this for several reasons. One is that I don't want to come to God with an entitlement attitude, as if something is owed to me. Before I was saved, I was a sinner who deserved death. I was saved through the life of God's son, Jesus Christ. It was a free gift. Therefore, I am owed nothing. I deserve nothing. I approach it all as being thankful for what I have, starting with my relationship with God.

One of my favorite sayings is, "What if I only had today what I thanked God for yesterday?" Would I have much? I think I would be OK because I thank God daily for my wife, my health, my children, my job, my life.

I view modern society as a whole and think: *Where are our manners?* My parents taught me to say "thank you" anytime someone did something for me. Why should that be any different for what God has done for me?

> *Give thanks to the Lord and proclaim his greatness.*
> *Let the whole world know what he has done.*
>
> 1 Chronicles 16:8 NLT

> *Be thankful in all circumstances, for this is God's will for you who belong to Christ Jesus.*
>
> 1 Thessalonians 5:18 NLT

We need to be thankful for where we are in our financial journey. Even if things are a mess and we are barely making it at the moment, we need to be thankful.

Do you realize that the poorest people in America are still better off than 99% of the world? We are privileged and blessed. We need to be thankful for the opportunities God has provided for us, especially in the area of our market-driven economy. We can look for better jobs and make more money through our initiative. In many countries, that does not exist.

> *Give thanks to the Lord, for he is good! His faithful love endures forever.*

Psalm 136:1 NLT

God is good, a good provider, and we need to give thanks to him and all he does.

> *But among you there must not be even a hint of sexual immorality, or of any kind of impurity, or of greed, because these are improper for God's holy people. Nor should there be obscenity, foolish talk or coarse joking, which are out of place, but rather thanksgiving.*

Ephesians 5:3 NIV

Two things I notice in this scripture. We shouldn't have a hint of greed, and we should replace such sins with being thankful.

> *Then Jesus took the loaves, gave thanks to God, and distributed them to the people. Afterward he did the same with the fish. And they all ate as much as they wanted.*

John 6:11 NLT

Have you ever noticed that when Jesus prayed for a meal, all he did was give thanks for it? He didn't pray for the lost; he didn't pray for a healing; he didn't pray for safe travels; he didn't pray "bless the hands that made it and make it fit for our bodies." (How could he miss that one?) He just gave thanks. Nothing wrong with praying all those things, but we should first give thanks for the food and God's provision.

We need to become a people who thank God for everything.

I encourage you to start thanking God for what you have, even if it isn't what you want or even the best you were hoping for. Be thankful for what you have, and watch God give the increase.

Thankfulness opens doors to God's blessing.

Enter his gates with thanksgiving
and his courts with praise;
give thanks to him and praise his name.
For the Lord is good and his love endures forever;
his faithfulness continues through all generations.

Psalm 100:4-5 NIV

I have found my attitude is much better when I am thankful and not entitled. In fact, on days where I get a little down or stressed, I start listing the things I am thankful for: my wife, my children, my job, a roof over my head, a free country and BBC's *Top Gear*. In no time, my attitude improves. Why don't you try it? It's free. It certainly can't hurt.

My last thought on thankfulness is one of my favorite sayings:

It's not happy people who are thankful.
It's thankful people that are happy.

Wealth doesn't make you happy. Being thankful makes you happy. I am thankful to God for blessing me financially, but the finances aren't what makes me happy. It's being thankful.

Thank you, Jesus!

15

Final Thoughts

OVER THE YEARS, people have asked me: "What made you so successful? How can I be as successful as you are?"

My answer is always the same: God created us to make wealth. I was created to be a financer of the Kingdom. Quite possibly you were as well.

I wrote this book to follow my response with the five keys essential for making wealth. God is calling many people to make wealth and be financers of the Kingdom. As we take the position of being stewards, becoming givers, worshiping God and not money, and keeping our eyes on Jesus, God will honor and entrust us with more. Father God will say:

> *Well done, good and faithful servant! You have been faithful with a few things; I will put you in charge of many things. Come and share your master's happiness!*

Matthew 25:23 NIV

I want to encourage you to check your motives concerning wealth. If following God's principles is just so you can have more toys, it probably won't work. However, if it is to be closer to God, to know him, honor him and further his Kingdom, it will definitely work.

When we become stewards of more, however, we must press deeper into God. It is tempting to gain a little success, think we have arrived, and grow independent of God. When things are tough, we cry out to God, but when things are good, we tend to forget him. Yet I would rather have nothing and know God than have all the money in the world and not know God.

From Deuteronomy:

> *When you have eaten and are satisfied, praise the Lord your God for the good land he has given you. Be careful that you do not forget the Lord your God, failing to observe his commands, his laws and his decrees that I am giving you this day. Otherwise, when you eat and are satisfied, when you build fine houses and settle down, and when your herds and flocks grow large and your silver and gold increase and all you have is multiplied, then your heart will become proud and you will forget the Lord your God, who brought you out of Egypt, out of the land of slavery.*

> Deuteronomy 8:10-14 NIV

God is warning us not to forget him when we are comfortable, when we have a nice house, money in the bank, a car or two, first-class vacations and whatever other stuff we may desire. We must remain dependent on God and continue to press into him...in good times and tough times.

Diligently pursue God. Don't take your eyes off of him. He is the prize, not the material things.

> *In this way, King Hezekiah handled the distribution throughout all Judah, doing what was pleasing and good in the sight of the Lord his God. In all that he did in the service of the Temple of God and in his efforts to follow God's laws and commands,*

Hezekiah sought his God wholeheartedly. As a result, he was very successful.

2 Chronicles 31:20 NLT (emphasis added)

Hezekiah sought God wholeheartedly. Likewise, we need to seek God wholeheartedly no matter where we are in our finances. When we have scant resources, we need to seek God. When we have abundant resources, we need to seek God.

Don't make your living by extortion or put your hope in stealing. And if your wealth increases, don't make it the center of your life.

Psalm 62:10 NLT

The word is cautioning us to not make money our main focus. Keep the right perspective and don't let it become mammon.

The Bible mentions money or finances over 800 times, and Jesus spoke of the same in most of his parables. Wealth, our attitude toward it and how we steward it, must be important to God for him to speak about it so much.

Will you become intentional with your finances and how you view them? You may need to repent and ask God to give you a godly perspective of wealth.

Money is the main thing married couples fight over. I have seen this in the people around me. This stress could be eliminated if we had the right perspective of money and applied the five keys I have laid out. If you're married, re-read this book together so both of you are on the same page.

I will leave you with one last thought. Robert Herjavec said, "A goal without a timeline is just a dream." Without assigning a start and finish time to a goal, it will not materialize. You need to decide when you will change and how you will implement these five keys to meet your goals.

My prayer is that this book will revolutionize your life, that you will acquire a godly perspective of wealth. I pray there will be a transfer of wealth to you. I pray God will be your God, not mammon.

Keep God first in all things.

About the Author

BOB BERTELSEN HAS OVER 30 YEARS IN BUSINESS and founded his current company, A Plus Powder Coaters, Inc., in 1996.

He has worked diligently to develop a great culture in his company where the employees have established the values of respect, attitude and quality. A Plus Powder Coaters, Inc., was named Business of the Year in 2016 by the Columbiana Ohio Chamber of Commerce. Bob credits this award to his employees for their values and culture. Bob mentors several businessmen, helping them establish Godly principles in their companies. He currently sits on the Custom Coaters Steering Committee for PCI (Powder Coaters Institute) and served as a director to the Columbiana Chamber of Commerce for many years.

One of Bob's passions is being a good steward, something that has been on his heart for over 25 years. He has spoken at various churches and seminars on stewardship, giving and finances. Bob considers himself, a "Financer of the Kingdom," a person created to make wealth to partner with ministries to fund their needs.

In his spare time, Bob races and builds vintage race cars. He currently is racing a 1968 Corvette, and nationally is in second place in points.

Bob and his wife, Laurie, currently reside in Columbiana, Ohio. They have three adult daughters. Bob and Laurie are a part of Real Living Ministries in Boardman, Ohio.

Bob can be reached at his website:

finishlineresources.com

Resources

Thank you for reading my book. Here some of the things you'll find on the website: finishlineresources.com

- Home "Decree of Ownership"

- Business "Decree of Ownership"

- Audio files

- Videos

- Pictures of the fire in 1988

- Information on Bob Bertelsen

- More about Bob's Racing

- Updates on new books and resources

- Contact info for speaking engagements

Help Us Reach Others

Thank you for reading my book, *Created to Make Wealth*. If you have enjoyed this book and feel it has been helpful, would you take the time to go to Amazon.com and write a review? The review will help others see the value in this book and allow more people to have the opportunity create wealth.

Made in the USA
Columbia, SC
04 March 2025